ABOLITION!

Richard S. Reddie was born in Bradford, West Yorkshire to Jamaican parents. He first took an interest in slavery after watching the docudrama, *Roots*, as a ten-year-old. He subsequently studied Spanish and Caribbean Studies at degree level which enabled him to travel extensively throughout the Caribbean and Latin America to assess the historical impact of slavery on these diverse societies. After taking a Masters degree in Information Management, he has written for a number of publications and edited *Focus*, the quarterly publication of the African Caribbean Evangelical Alliance.

He is currently the Project Director of **set all free**, the Churches Together in England campaign, which looks to highlight the significance of the bicentenary of the abolition of the Slave Trade Act.

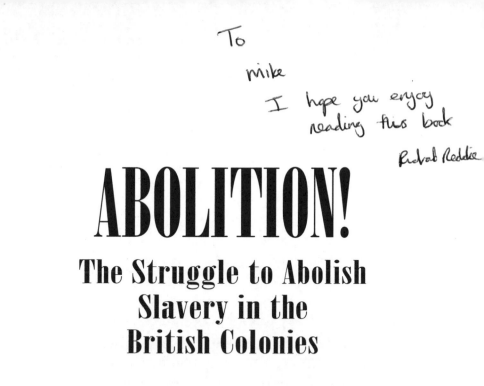

To
mike
I hope you enjoy
reading this book
Richard Reddie

ABOLITION!

The Struggle to Abolish
Slavery in the
British Colonies

Richard S. Reddie

LION

I dedicate this book to my darling wife, Lilian, whose advice, encouragement and inspiration were paramount to the book's emergence. Whenever I was down, she pulled me up.

I also dedicate this book to my son, Noah Luke Reddie. Tomorrow's world belongs to him. Let's hope it's one where all are set free.

Contents

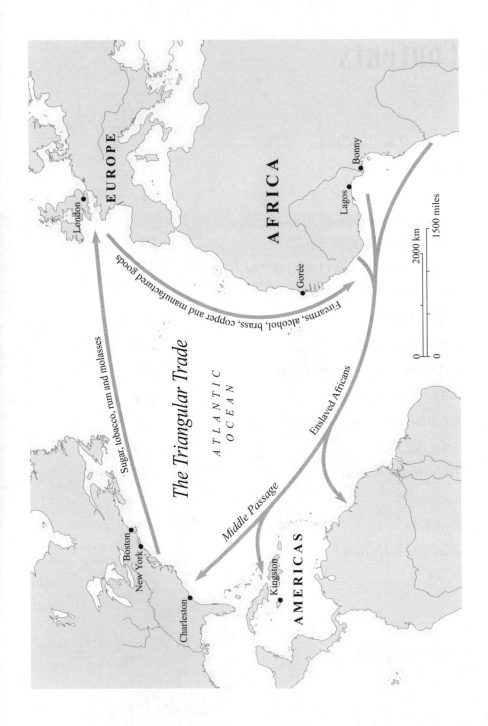

The Triangular Trade

ATLANTIC
OCEAN

EUROPE

London

AFRICA

Bonny

Lagos

Gorée

Firearms, alcohol, brass, copper and manufactured goods

Enslaved Africans

Sugar, tobacco, rum and molasses

Boston

New York

Charleston

Middle Passage

Kingston

AMERICAS

2000 km

1500 miles

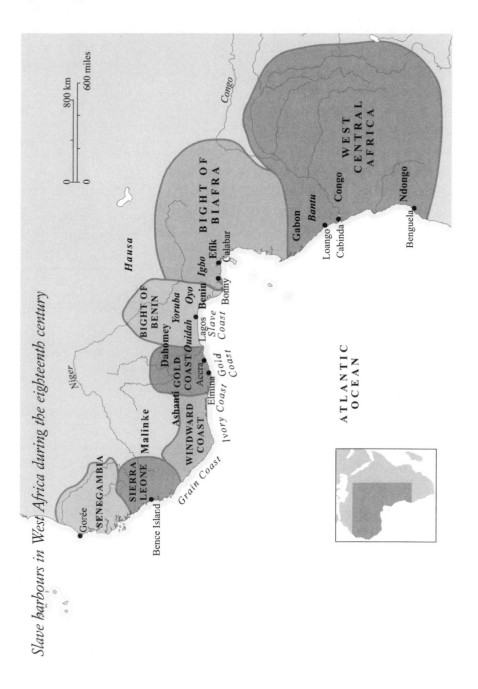

Slave harbours in West Africa during the eighteenth century

Foreword

This is a scholarly, readable and timely book published as we remember the bicentenary of the 1807 act of parliament, which marked an important stage in the long battle to abolish slavery.

Unlike most other accounts of the campaign, Richard Reddie identifies the role of Africans themselves in helping to achieve their own liberation while also revealing the ambivalent role of the Christian churches, some of which were interested in converting the slaves while others denounced the trade uncompromisingly.

Abolition! also emphasizes the economic factors which helped make slavery so profitable and traces these profits back to those in England who made great fortunes, as in my own constituency in Bristol. Here, some slave traders are now remembered as benefactors and until recently, many people of the City of Bristol seemed reluctant to admit the role played in the slave trade. The sheer brutality and inhumanity associated with slavery was accepted for far too long because it enriched so many influential people.

The author pays tribute to the Quakers, William Wilberforce, Thomas Clarkson and Olaudah Equiano, the latter a freed slave who campaigned passionately in both England and the colonies for the ending of the trade. The colonies and their slave owners clung on to their right to own slaves for many decades before, in the end, being compensated instead of the slaves themselves.

Reddie draws particular attention to the exploitation of Africa through the theft of its oil, copper, diamonds and gold reserves by corrupt traders, and notes that the 2005 G8 summit in Gleneagles did not include proper African representation when a new trade policy was drafted. Indeed, we still ask the wrong question, 'why are the poor poor?', instead of asking 'why are the rich rich?'. Compensation for those many millions of African slaves who were shipped to the 'New World' might best be achieved by unilaterally abolishing all debts owed by African governments.

Richard Reddie's excellent book should remind us that the battles he describes so brilliantly have to be fought and won again and again by each generation.

Tony Benn

Preface

In this account of transatlantic slavery and its abolition I have adopted a holistic approach which makes a fulsome connection between Europe, Africa and the Americas. These three regions were inextricably linked to the Transatlantic Slave Trade, and not to explore their particular histories, both before and during slavery, denies the reader a context in which to explore the impact of these events. In particular, I explore the histories of Africa and the Americas, prior to and during the slave trade, to re-emphasize this link between Europe, Africa and the Americas.

I have also used this holistic approach in relation to the abolition movement in order to explore the role of Africans themselves in the history of the Transatlantic Slave Trade. An extraordinary feature of the recounting of transatlantic slavery is the way Africans have been sidelined from their own history. The Transatlantic Slave Trade was all about the enslavement and emancipation of Africans, and yet up until recently, very few historians even mentioned the names of those Africans who fought to end slavery. Some academics tended to present Africans as passive victims of slavery who waited for God and white men to deliver them from enslavement. Historical studies, however, reveal that Africans were largely the agents of their own freedom and worked alongside their European counterparts to end slavery in all its forms.

Equally, nearly all history books describe Africans as 'slaves' and little else and it is not uncommon to see a book entitled 'the Freeing of the Slaves'. Given the international nature of slavery (practically every country in the world practised slavery at one time or another) and the fact that the system is as old as time, I prefer to use the term 'enslaved African(s)', wherever possible, for greater clarification and accuracy. This is particularly important when discussing the Transatlantic Slave Trade because at various times both whites and indigenous people were also used as 'slaves', so it is important to make it clear who is being enslaved and who is carrying out the enslaving.

I also try to use the term 'enslaved African' to show that slavery is a status imposed on an individual. The majority of Africans were enslaved. Prior to their enslavement they were men and women with families who held down a variety of jobs and lived normal lives. The Transatlantic Slave Trade ruined this. To solely use the term 'slave' then is to collude with the oppressive system that sought to rob Africans of their individuality and humanity.

Starting with Eric Williams' seminal book *Capitalism and Slavery* in 1944, the recent tendency of historians has been to play down the role of altruism in abolition, especially that of a religious nature. Unlike them, however, I have paid particular attention to the role of religion, both positive and negative, in the instigation and cessation of the Transatlantic Slave Trade. It is interesting that during the late eighteenth and then nineteenth century, Britain underwent a religious revival. It also had the most organized abolitionist movement, which was born out of religious conviction. It is my contention, therefore, that there was a clear link between such conviction and social action and it is worth comparing – or contrasting – the British scenario with that of France. At the same time as Britain was forming abolition committees, France was in the first throes of revolutionary fervour, making protestations about liberty, equality and fraternity. However, France's involvement in the anti-slavery movement comes a poor second to Britain's and I would argue that the lack of a clear religious dimension to French life was the reason for this lack of activity.

I am aware that in writing this book, I am attempting to address a hugely significant and emotional event in the history of both Britain and the whole of Western civilization. The Transatlantic Slave Trade exerted a huge impact on the social, cultural, political and economic development of the world.

I am also cognisant of the emotional and political sensitivities linked to this subject. For many, particularly those of African descent, engaging with the memory and legacies of slavery is no mere academic subject or dispassionate form of intellectual undertaking. Rather, slavery represents a deep struggle in the psyche of many people. As such, no one text can ever attempt to satisfy the plethora of interests and liberationist struggles for justice and equality that arise from all who wish to remember the 200th anniversary of the British parliamentary act to abolish the slave trade. I know that this book will not satisfy the competing demands of people wanting to remember and commemorate the actions of eighteenth-and-nineteenth century abolitionists, both black or white.

Given that my work cannot be all things to all people, I have been forced to take a particular position in order to make sense of this problematic and crucial period within British history.* While I have made every attempt to undertake this task in an objective and rational way, it would be naive to claim that my own perspectives and feelings have not helped shape this undertaking. This approach has been influenced by my own

---

* I have chosen to use the term English/England in certain sections of this book, as opposed to Britain, because prior to 1603, and especially before the Acts of Union in 1707, Britain (or, to give the full name, the kingdom of Great Britain) did not exist as either a legal or a parliamentary entity.

background, upbringing and religious faith. I am an African (Caribbean) British subject who was raised in a Christian household and who remains a member of the Christian church. My approach to detailing the development and ultimate end of slavery has, therefore, been undertaken from a black Atlantic, Caribbean Christian perspective.

I cannot write for all people nor pretend to be a disinterested observer.

Richard S. Reddie

Introduction

The bicentenary of the abolition of the Slave Trade Act has presented Britain and the rest of the world with an opportunity to reassess the impact and legacy of the forced transportation of Africans from their continent to toil in the Americas for the financial benefit of Europe. The anniversary has also given us a unique opportunity to examine the efforts of heroic abolitionists to end Britain's involvement in transatlantic slavery. Historical studies reveal that Britain (or England at the time) first dabbled in slave trading in the mid-sixteenth century and ended its involvement only three centuries later. The story of Britain's participation in the Transatlantic Slave Trade is one of greed, violence, exploitation and expedition. But it is also an account of courage, shame, toil and, ultimately, triumph, which explores all that is good and sometimes rotten with the human condition.

For some people of African origin, the Transatlantic Slave Trade ranks alongside the Holocaust as one of the darkest episodes in human history, and yet there is no collective sorrow or lament over how it was allowed to persist for so long. The figures connected to the slave trade are both incredible and ghastly; anywhere between 9–15 million Africans were forcibly transported from their continent to the Americas over several centuries. In fact, the Transatlantic Slave Trade still remains one of the largest forced movements of human beings the world has ever witnessed. However, unlike the Holocaust, which is often blamed on the machinations of an evil megalomaniac and the warped political ideology of one country, virtually the whole of Europe at that time was involved in the slave trade, and this perhaps is one of the reasons for the absence of a shared international response in remembering what some call the African Holocaust or MAAFA.*

Moreover, the so-called legacies of the Transatlantic Slave Trade are equally astounding. It is estimated that over 100 million people of African descent live in the Americas today and the ancestors of at least 90 per cent of them arrived on slavers (slave ships). Likewise, such was the sustained nature of slave trading that many countries in the Caribbean and elsewhere in the region today have majority African populations, such as Brazil whose fondness for slave trading ensures that its population has more people of African origin than any other country in the world except for Nigeria.

But if the statistics are astounding and appear almost unparalleled within human history, the questions remain of why slavery is still today a footnote on a page of world history and why it is still primarily the preserve of academics or black studies. I have suggested that the collective involvement of European countries is a factor, but there is no doubt that it goes much deeper than this. Perhaps the real answer lies in the fact that the enslavement of African people remains a highly emotive subject, one which most people prefer to ignore or overlook out of a sense of shame, pain, anger or fear.

Some argue that it 'happened a long time ago and we should draw a line under it and move on', but when slavery is discussed in public forums today, one can always guarantee heated debates and forthright discussions. Certainly, for some in the black community, the Transatlantic Slave Trade remains unfinished business and its consequences not only impact the societies in which we live, but also have a continuing emotionalor psychological effect on people of African origin.

* MAAFA is a Kiswahili term for 'disaster' or 'terrible occurrence'.

Indeed, several academics argue that some black people still suffer the effects of what is classified as Post-Traumatic Slave Syndrome in which the legacy of slavery remains etched within black people's souls. They claim that 'understanding the role our past plays in our present attitudes, outlooks, mindsets and circumstances is important if we are to free ourselves from the spiritual, mental and emotional shackles that bind us today, shackles that limit what we believe we can be, do and have today'.[1]

The debate about the apparent continuing emotional damage to individuals finds its equivalent in arguments about the way the Transatlantic Slave Trade 'under-developed' the continent of Africa and the numerous countries within the former British West Indies (now known as the Caribbean). These issues, allied to the fact that Europe undoubtedly benefited financially from the Transatlantic Slave Trade, have led to calls in some quarters for an apology 'of substance' and/or reparations.*

Another palpable legacy of the Transatlantic Slave Trade – some would argue the greatest legacy – has been the racism that continues to blight societies and has condemned many of African descent to marginal roles within the countries that either practised or exported slavery. Again, numerous debates have taken place about how societies can end the prejudices and discrimination that have outlived the Transatlantic Slave Trade and the bicentenary has brought these issues sharply back into focus.

I contend, however, that such is the lack of knowledge about the Transatlantic Slave Trade that we cannot assume anything with regard to what most people know about slavery. Slavery has been expunged from society's frame of reference out of a

---

* Unlike the United States, the reparations debate in the UK is relatively new and many are still grappling with what constitutes reparations. Some suggest it carries financial implications while others argue that it has more to do with repairing the damage that was caused by the slave trade to African people and their societies.

collective sense of guilt, ensuring that a lot of the information found in this book will be completely new to many readers. It is arguable that the brave men and women who worked to end chattel enslavement (absolute legal ownership of a person or persons, including the legal right to buy or sell them) have been deliberately written out of history because of their connection to this sensitive subject. As a consequence, figures who should be celebrated and acknowledged in both Britain and the wider world for their sterling work are barely known today. Even the most celebrated abolitionist, William Wilberforce, is not that well known in Britain, and yet his efforts easily match those of Horatio Nelson or the Duke of Wellington, men of a similar era but known throughout the world for their respective pursuits.

One of the real tasks in raising awareness of Britain's historical participation in slavery involves helping people to understand the clear difference between the termination of Britain's involvement in the slave trade in 1807 and the cessation of transatlantic slavery in 1833. This is pretty straightforward and yet *The Times* newspaper, no less, made the common error of confusing the end of the slave trade and slavery itself in its article 'If only Britain had thought of something like the Magna Carta'.[2] This highlights the general lack of knowledge about a subject that played an integral part in the socio-economic development of Britain as a country.

The bicentenary has also focused many minds on people trafficking, which is considered to be the modern-day equivalent of the slave trade. Indeed, there are certain similarities between the two with regard to the degrading exploitation involved in the transportation of men, women and children between countries and continents. Trafficking is a worldwide phenomenon affecting millions and as a consequence many groups are working to end this abuse throughout the world.

I would contend, however, that it would be wrong to make direct comparisons between the Transatlantic Slave Trade and people trafficking. The first reason is that the trafficking of people, like other forms of modern slavery, is illegal. There are numerous international conventions, laws and protocols that outlaw this practice. The main issue associated with people trafficking is whether the various governments of this world have a vested interest in enforcing these laws. The Transatlantic Slave Trade, however, remained legal for centuries and was only outlawed in the nineteenth century.

The second and equally subtle difference between the two is that people trafficking is not only illegal, but it is also regarded as despicable. The trafficking of people is placed in the same bracket as drugs smuggling, arms dealing or counterfeiting. When most 'decent, law-abiding folk' are told about the existence of people trafficking, they invariably ask how this can happen in our enlightened society and suggest that the government ought to do something about it. Equally, law-abiding activists will enquire about how they can work with groups and organizations to end this human cruelty. This was not the situation with the slave trade which, according to the author Philippa Gregory was a respectable trade.[3]

In fact, various kings, queens and other members of the royal family were involved in the Transatlantic Slave Trade, as were members of the aristocracy and the church. The Transatlantic Slave Trade was a business that involved the great and the good because it was both lucrative and took place overseas, so it was possible for investors to ignore the sufferings of Africans and focus simply on the profits that they could make from this venture.

The people trafficking/slave-trading debate also partially reduces the efforts of the abolitionists who over 200 years ago were working to change hearts and minds about the evils of the slave trade and the humanity of Africans. They faced a system that argued that the slave trade was financially advantageous for Britain, and structures which used religious and philosophical ideas to justify African enslavement.

Today though, many are left wondering how and why our forebears took so long to realize that it was wrong to treat fellow human beings in such a callous way. We do not need to do any similar soul searching with people trafficking because it is roundly condemned by most, and various groups are urging the governments of the world to concentrate their efforts on arresting the traffickers and protecting the victims.

Instead, we need to think 'outside the box' for something comparable to the slave trade. This would be an activity or practice that is currently legal and which many support, putting forward a range of arguments in order to justify it. It would also be something that others oppose today for moral or ethical reasons, but our descendants in 100 or 200 years time may question why it was ever allowed to take place. This could be, for example, current economic practices or animal testing.

We should also concentrate hearts and minds on other forms of modern slavery such as debt bondage, slavery by descent, forced labour and the unconditional forms of child labour, which condemn millions to servitude around the world. If the historic face of slavery was largely an African one, the contemporary face has a variety of complexions and is a worldwide issue. It is important to draw on lessons from the original abolition movement to end modern slavery, not only for inspiration but to ensure that we do not make the same mistakes. While the first abolitionists did sterling work to help end slavery, they ignored the systems and structures that contributed to the enslavement of Africans. As a consequence, the lives of the newly emancipated Africans in the British West

Indies were little improved after slavery was abolished in the 1830s. Although the Africans were no longer physical slaves, they were enslaved by a system that considered them second-class citizens and denied them the right to fully participate in the running of their countries. The efforts to end modern slavery must therefore focus on dismantling structures that contribute to enslavement so that newly-freed slaves are not forced back into something that is still slavery in all but name.

1

Crossing Continents: Africa before the Transatlantic Slave Trade

'Perhaps in the future there will be some African history to teach. But at present there is none, or very little: there is only the history of Europe in Africa.'

The one-time Regius Professor of History at Oxford University, Hugh Trevor Roper (later Lord Dacre), made these infamous comments about Africa in 1963. In doing so, his ill-informed views helped to reinforce the long-established belief that African history began with European exploration and the Transatlantic Slave Trade. Fortunately, other historians such as John Henrik Clarke, Basil Davidson and Cheikh Anta Diop have debunked this misconception and have argued that the continent had a rich, diverse history long before the arrival of the first Europeans.

Far too often, however, books on the African or Transatlantic Slave Trade begin with the arrival of the first Europeans and fail to provide any background on the continent before this. Even when they do, it is only to look at indigenous or Arab slavery or the place of slavery in world history. But without this analysis, it is impossible to assess the full socio-economic and cultural impact of the slave trade on the continent and its people – the issue at the heart of the ongoing debates about African underdevelopment and reparations. There is little doubt that it would be remiss of a historian to discuss the Norman invasion of England in 1066 without giving an account of Saxon life before William of Normandy's arrival. Consequently, when history programmes discuss '1066 and all that', the 'all that' includes what took place both before and after the Conquest.

In the case of Africa, it is vitally important to put the slave trade into the context of African history overall, offering an African BC and AD, which provides a before, during and after analysis. This would not only ensure an accurate assessment of the Transatlantic Slave Trade, but would also bring in the colonization that followed the ending of slavery in the colonies. Without this, the important intellectual debates between academics such as Walter Rodney and David Eltis[1] lose a great deal of their validity.

An accurate account of African history, both pre- and post-slavery, is vitally important because the Western world has been responsible for a series of misleading notions about Africa. These began with the tales of early European travellers who explored the so-called 'dark continent' during the age of expedition and continued with the colonials who governed most of the huge continent after the scramble for Africa in the nineteenth century. A much more recent factor in shaping opinion has been Hollywood, the centre of the mainstream American movie industry.

Films can be used for a variety of purposes; the 'propaganda' movies during the Second World War helped to spur on the Allies' war efforts against the Nazis and the Japanese. A more negative usage of the power of cinema, however, has been the making of numerous Hollywood films (especially during its golden age in the 1920s to 1940s) that portrayed Africa as a savage and dangerous place full of jungles and cannibals. Indeed, international box office smashes such as *King Solomon's Mines* and the perennial *Tarzan* movies developed stereotypes and caricatures that still live on in people's minds today. Africa was the place where Europeans 'go native' and finish up corrupted by its primitiveness and savagery. Similarly, it was an area in need of civilizing and educating after centuries of slavery, slave trading, war, animism and cannibalism.

This unbalanced view of Africa does not concur with scientific opinion, which suggests that human life began in Africa and that the continent was the cradle of civilization. The Great Nubian civilization, in what is now southern Egypt and northern Sudan, was known for its gold, ivory, stone, ebony and incense, which was traded with neighbours. The Nubians were great fighting people – their civilization or kingdom was known as the 'land of the bow' and many Nubian men served as palace guards or warriors in other African kingdoms.

The Egyptians, who were famed for their Pharaohs, were capable of incredible technical and scientific feats and the world is indebted to them today in the fields of medicine, mathematics, philosophy and the arts. It is now also argued by some academics that ancient Africa's influence on Europe can be seen through its effect on Greek intellectuals who were influenced by the developments that took place in Egypt. For instance, the renowned Greek scholars Archimedes and Pythagoras studied in Egypt prior to making their names in mathematics. They were also equipped in the humanities and during the fifth century BC, Herodotus considered them 'the best historians of any nation of which I have experienced'.[2]

Great developments also took place in sub-Saharan Africa with civilizations such as Great Zimbabwe, Ghana, Songhay and Mali enjoying centuries of economic prosperity and social cohesion. Sub-Saharan Africa shared many of the technological developments found in the north and according to the Senegalese academic, Cheikh Anta Diop, 'the use of metallurgy in black Africa dates back to time immemorial'.[3] There is also evidence that East Africans were producing steel in carbon furnaces many centuries before Europe.

In the west of Africa, the kingdom of Ghana extended into a vast empire between the ninth and thirteenth centuries. It occupied local chieftaincies and generated great wealth from its trade in gold, salt, copper, and even human beings between Western Africa and the Middle East via Egypt. In his *Kitab fi Masalik wal Mamalik* (The Book of Roads and Kingdoms), the Spanish–Muslim geographer Al-Bakri described tenth-century Ghana as a 'highly advanced, economically prosperous country'. Indeed, the Ghanaian sovereign reputedly had a military numbering 200,000 men and his empire spread across an area roughly the size of Western Europe.

The Ghanaian sovereign had a liking for gold and 'he, his heir apparent and the notables all literally dripped with gold. The pages, horses and dogs… were equally covered with it. People were literally living in gold…'.[4] Ghana became an iron-using state around AD 700 and it was this technological development that enabled the kingdom to dominate her neighbours. According to El Zouhi, the eleventh-century Arab chronicler, 'most West African people know not iron and fight with bars of ebony' and the people of Ghana 'defeat them because they fight with swords and lances'.[5]

The kingdom of Mali became the next major African force after the decline of Ghana in the thirteenth century, dominating parts of West and North-East Africa until the fifteenth century. Mali seized control of the gold, salt and caravan trades between the west and the north of the continent and also cornered the trade in copper, exploiting the mines that lay to the east of its growing empire. Around AD 1300, Ibn Battuta, the Moroccan-born medieval traveller, described the Africans in Mali as 'seldom unjust, and [they] have a greater abhorrence of injustice than any other people. Their Sultan shows no mercy to anyone who is found guilty of the least act of it. There is complete security in the country. Neither traveller nor inhabitant in it has anything to fear from robbers or men of violence. They do not confiscate the property of any white man who dies in their country, even if it be uncounted wealth. On the contrary they give it into the charge of some trustworthy person among the whites, until the rightful heir takes possession of it'.[6]

A careful analysis of African history reveals that as one kingdom teetered on the brink of collapse, another often emerged and this was the situation between the kingdoms of Mali and Songhay (or Songhai). The Songhay, which was the most powerful West African state between 1450–1550, would eclipse the kingdom of Mali during the sovereignty of King Sonni Ali. He reigned from 1464–92 and under his expansionist rule would expel the Berbers (Afro-Asiatic-speaking people who originally inhabited Egypt, Algeria and Libya, and who followed Islam) and conquer the cities of Timbuktu and Jenné.

Under the rule of his successor, Askia Muhammad Touré (1493–1528), the vast Songhay empire underwent conversion to Islam to tighten the ruler's grip on power. But as well as making Islam the official religion of the empire, Touré also introduced standardization of weights, measures and currency, as well as centralized government with a complex bureaucratic system. By the fifteenth century, the legendary city of Timbuktu had become the hub of the written tradition in Africa and one of the continent's main seats of learning. Timbuktu was also the location of Sankore Mosque, also known as the University of Sankore, which had assembled a formidable group of scholars, professors and lecturers unrivalled in Africa.

Such was the renown of Timbuktu that an old West African proverb recalling the glories of the city proposed, 'Salt comes from the north, gold from the south, but the word of God and the treasures of wisdom come from Timbuktu.' Moreover, El Hasan ben Muhammed el-Wazzan-ez-Zayyati, better known as Leo Africanus, the sixteenth-century Moroccan adventurer, provided a vivid account of Timbuktu life in 1526. He described the city's inhabitants as 'very rich' and noted that 'fabrics are imported from Europe'.[7]

African and Arab views on African kingdoms were comparable to those of their European counterparts of the time. As Europeans began to explore the vast continent, beginning initially in North and West Africa, traders and explorers provided insightful journal entries describing what they encountered on their travels. A common feature of most diary records was the comparison between African kingdoms and those in Europe at the time. A Dutch explorer visiting the West African kingdom of Dahomey (modern-day Benin) in the early seventeenth century provided a telling assessment of the capital.

He wrote, 'It looks very big when you enter it for you go into a great broad street, which, though not paved, seems to be seven or eight times broader than the Warmoes Street in Amsterdam... Outside the gate there is a large suburb. Inside as you go along the main street, you can see other broad streets on either side, and these are also straight. The houses in this town stand in good order, one close to the other and evenly placed beside the next, like our houses in Holland.'[8] Similarly, the sixteenth-century Portuguese trader Duarte Barbosa described the East African city of Kilwa as having 'many fair houses of stone and mortar, well arranged streets. Around it were streams and orchards with many channels of sweet water'.[9]

Both accounts highlight the fact that West and East Africa were by no means inferior to Europe from a cultural or technological standpoint. Africa had its centres of learning, discrediting theories that it only had an 'oral' tradition, without the capacity to record its history. The continent was also in possession of ideas and theories that were being constantly exchanged among its various kingdoms and cultures.

It is something of a paradox, therefore, that the early European explorers would provide such gushing, flattering accounts of African kingdoms yet still use terms such as 'uncivilized' or 'primitive' to describe the people who built them. However, Africa is not alone in this apparent contradiction and it is good to compare the early accounts of African exploration with the Spanish conquest of Mexico by Hernán Cortés and his conquistadores in 1518.

Cortés described the Aztec capital, Tenochtitlán, as a 'great city... built on the salt lake, and no matter by what road you travel there are two leagues from the main body of the city to the mainland. There are four artificial causeways leading to it, and each is as wide as two cavalry lances. The city itself is as big as Seville or Córdoba... They are all very beautiful buildings... Amongst these temples there is one, the principal one, whose great size and magnificence no human tongue could describe, for it is so large that within the precincts, which are surrounded by a very high wall, a town of some five hundred inhabitants could easily be built.'[10]

Although Cortés used such flowing language to describe this amazing city, he chose to destroy it when he set about pacifying the Aztecs. European adventurers had a tendency to compare and contrast everything they saw on their travels and yet many were 'men of their time' who, when confronted by unfamiliar ideas or practices, tended to dismiss them as primitive or evil and sought to destroy them. Cortés rebuilt Mexico City in the style of a Spanish city.

The history of Africa, prior to European conquest, is important for a number of reasons. It shows that something happened both during and after the fifteenth century to significantly stunt development in many parts of the continent. Historians such as the Guyanese academic Walter Rodney argue that the Transatlantic Slave Trade was the catalyst for this decline, and his opinions are echoed by Basil Davidson who argued that the slave trade 'cut savagely across those many complex strands of commerce which centuries had woven between these myriad ports and peoples... and wrecked the whole fabric of that trade, leaving behind... little but ruin and disruption'.[11]

This abridged walk through African history also shows that Africans, especially those in West Africa who suffered the most from the Transatlantic Slave Trade, were civilized, organized, and to some degree industrialized peoples, long before any European had time to suggest they were backward peoples. However, the debate many academics are still having is the extent to which the discrimination faced by Africans, both during and after enslavement, arose as a result of racism. The Caribbean academic Eric Williams argued that 'slavery caused racism, but economic motives not racial ideas caused slavery'.[12] In Williams' opinion, the decision to enslave Africans and keep them in lifelong bondage was inextricably linked to the rise of plantation slavery in the West Indies and the need for cheap labour. Williams stated that Europeans finally settled on Africans after using and discarding white labourers, and that

31

Indian and Chinese workers would have fitted the bill had those areas been closer to Europe than Africa.

Conversely, Winthrop D. Jordan claimed that although economics played an important role in African enslavement, the 'religious, physical and cultural differences' that distinguished Europeans from Africans would eventually be seen in terms of colour.[13] For Winthrop Graham, many in Europe at this time – especially the English – viewed the colour black very negatively,* and the fact that Africans were black and few were Christians compounded the situation. Jordan does not suggest that these factors were a direct cause of African enslavement, but he does argue that they played a significant role.

Furthermore, the authors Terence Brady and Evan Jones write that, 'once slavery had been accepted both as an economic and as a social custom the black [African] was regarded increasingly as inferior. This belief started on the coast of Africa as white overseers and traders loaded the hundreds of blacks into the holds of the slave ships, and was fostered on the plantations. Blackness became synonymous with enslavement… once slave trading became a widely practised custom in the European countries, references start appearing about the "thick lipp'd slave" and the total inferiority of the Negro race'.[14]

Although the debate still rages as to whether 'racism' was the cause of African enslavement or a by-product, there is little doubt that the Transatlantic Slave Trade turned Africans from human beings into 'commodities' and 'cargo'. By 1562, the

---

* The word 'black' has always been a loaded term in the English language, connoting negativity. Some Christian Englishman at that time interpreted certain Bible verses as suggesting that black was the colour of sin, the devil and general wickedness. Conversely, everything pure and good was white. The English would adopt the Spanish/Portuguese term for black (Negro) and use it instead of the word 'African'.

English adventurer and slave trader, Sir John Hawkins, was using the term 'human cargo' to describe the 300 Africans he had seized during his first slave-trading venture. Others preferred the term 'commodities', but what is inescapable is the fact that Africans had stopped being 'human' in the eyes of many European explorers and traders and became chattel or moveable possessions.

Historical studies show that the first wave of European adventurers to Africa were leading men (and women) of their time. Akin to their counterparts in the Americas, issues of trade and exploration were uppermost in their minds. They also brought with them religious ideas that dismissed any beliefs and cultural practices that were not Christian. By the seventeenth century, Africans had stopped being people with curious religious practices and social customs and instead had become pagans and heathens who were 'two-legged' beasts or savages, found somewhere between humans and animals on the evolutionary scale. In many European minds, the Transatlantic Slave Trade was a 'godsend' that would save the Africans from the barbarity of their continent. It was pointed out that even the Atlantic currents from the West coast of Africa flowed in the right direction towards the West Indies providing Africans with a speedy route to salvation and civilization.

An old African proverb states that *'until lions have their own historians, the story of the hunt will always glorify the hunter'*. So it is with religion and the Transatlantic Slave Trade. Christianity was a key factor in the enslavement and transportation of Africans to the Americas. Traditionally, many tended to study the opinions of European travellers without examining the history of religion on the continent to query whether it was a region bereft of Christianity. Scholars now suggest that Christianity reached Africa no later than the early second century AD and that the Christian communities in North Africa were among the first in the world.

It has been argued also that the Christian faith was disseminated throughout parts of the African continent and northern Europe at more or less the same time. The New Testament provides an account of the Ethiopian official who was converted and baptized by the deacon Philip while travelling back from Jerusalem. According to David Brion Davis, St Menas, the patron saint of Alexandria, 'was sometimes depicted with "Negroid" features on the ampullae sold to pilgrims'.[15] He also points out that Ethiopian Christians were 'making pilgrimages to the Holy Land by the fourth century'.

By 1490, missionaries were plying their trade in southern Africa after King Nzinga of Kongo (in what is now northern Angola and most of the Congo) invited Catholic priests to share their beliefs among his people. Their work had the desired effect because the king converted to Catholicism, as did many of his subjects by default. King Nzinga would later send his son, Afonso, to Portugal to study for the ministry. When Afonso assumed the role of king after his father, Catholicism became entrenched in the kingdom and surrounding regions.

It has been suggested that Afonso's son, Henrique, would become the first indigenous African bishop in the Catholic Church. There is little doubt that Europeans encountered African Christians on their travels but refused to recognize the authenticity of their beliefs, as Christianity appeared incompatible with the cultural surroundings of the continent.

African religion, akin to the other social and technological developments in Africa, was deemed inferior by some Europeans, especially those who believed its people could teach them nothing and that it was instead a continent in need of everything that Europe had to offer. Such a closed mindset invariably results in condescension or patronization at best, or cruel exploitation or looting at worst. It also leads to the belief that people are ignorant or backward because they appear not to value what others would deem precious. For instance, the Europeans who first reached West Africa could not understand the nonchalance of the 'Gold Coast' Africans (what is now modern-day Ghana) to the gold deposits found in their region.

William St Clair suggests that 'rich African men and women wore gold ornaments... while African traders, often naked, except for a single cloth, carried gold dust in pouches tied to their legs'.[16] For many Europeans, gold was the 'be all and end all' and it underpinned the economies of most European countries. St Clair adds, 'The British in the Cape Coast Castle and forts accumulated gold dust in bottles in heavily locked closets, against the day when they could send it home and translate it into real wealth'.[17]

Indeed, all European explorers during the fifteenth and sixteenth centuries had gold on their minds while travelling to new worlds. We read that the notorious explorer Christopher Columbus, upon arriving in what is now the Bahamas during his first voyage to the New World, asked Native Americans where they had obtained the gold that adorned their bodies. They appeared confused as to why the Italian traveller was so fixated with the precious metal and pointed to other islands south of the Bahamas. Columbus wasted no time heading towards these destinations.

Over the centuries, European countries have fought to control Africa's natural resources such as gold, diamonds, oil, copper, bauxite, cocoa and mangetout as well as its lands. However, it can be argued that Europe first took a real interest in Africa during the Transatlantic Slave Trade when it looked to exploit the continent's most important primary resource, human beings. The Transatlantic Slave Trade would help to define Europe's relationship with Africa, which until only a few decades ago was firmly tilted in Europe's favour.

2

(Do you Remember) the Days of Slavery

In fourteen hundred and ninety two
Columbus sailed the ocean blue.

When everyone thought the world was flat,
Columbus said it's round.
He went down in history
When America was found.

There is little doubt that the Transatlantic Slave Trade is an account of the relationship between Europe, Africa and the Americas from the sixteenth to the nineteenth centuries. One could also argue that it was a tale of European capital (money and products), African labour (enslaved workers) and American commodities (sugar, tobacco, cotton). A prime mover in this infamous history was the Italian-born explorer Christopher Columbus, whom the authors Gail Cameron and Stan Crooke describe as the man who 'initiated the Transatlantic Slave Trade'.[1] Whether one can lay the blame for the Transatlantic Slave Trade on Columbus' shoulders is a matter for debate. What is not beyond doubt is the fact that he was the first person to argue the case for slavery in the Americas and was also a pioneer in the introduction of

European-style slavery to the Western Hemisphere.

Up until recently, history had been kind to Christopher Columbus and chose to remember him as the discoverer of the so-called New World, rather than as the father of slavery within the Americas.² It used to be the case that school children recited the famous rhyme that opened this chapter, mentioning exploits that involved Columbus persuading the king and queen of Spain (Ferdinand and Isabella) to sponsor his project of sailing west to reach the eastern countries of Cathay (China) and Cipangu (Japan).

Interestingly, prior to this agreement, Columbus had unsuccessfully tried to sell his idea to other European countries, and while on his travels he encountered enslaved Africans cultivating sugar cane on the Portuguese-run island of Madeira. It has been argued that the connection between sugar and slavery made a great impression on Columbus, and he would remember this as he made his four voyages to the Americas and shared numerous conversations with compatriots about how they could best develop the economies of the Americas.

On his first Spanish-sponsored journey in 1492, Columbus' journals reveal that he believed the 'Indians' he had met in what is now the Bahamas would make good slaves. Columbus invariably used the term 'Indian' to describe these would-be slaves because he mistakenly believed that he had reached Asia by way of the West. Consequently, he called the newly discovered territories the 'Indies' and its people 'Indians' and his error would remain with the region for centuries. It has only been in the last 40 years that the words 'West Indies' have been replaced with the term 'Caribbean' and 'Indian' with 'indigenous people' or 'Native American'. On his second journey to the Americas a year later, Columbus stopped off in the Canary Islands to collect samples of sugar cane. On his third voyage in 1498, he enslaved 600 indigenous people and sent them to Spain as presents to Queen Isabella, an act which saw the birth of the Transatlantic Slave Trade – in reverse.

Queen Isabella, like most Spaniards of the time, considered herself a good Catholic and was concerned about the spiritual welfare of the 'millions of unsaved savages' whom Columbus spoke about in the Indies. She immediately dispatched priests to accompany the administrators, soldiers and civilians whose duty it was to fashion the new territories into a Spanish-style kingdom in the Americas. The priests were assisted in their attempts to encourage the indigenous people to convert to Christianity by the introduction of laws which stated that any who refused would be enslaved.

There is little doubt that the 'discovery' of the Americas radically changed the way Europe saw the world. Columbus had shown the men of science that not only was the world indeed round, but that it was also a huge place with amazing resources ready for exploitation. After his first visit to the Americas, Columbus became the most famous and popular man in Spain. His renown even eclipsed the Spanish monarchy, something that no doubt displeased the king and queen. However, it was noticeable that after each voyage to the Americas his popularity decreased in direct proportion to the rise in suspicion and jealousy in many parts of the Spanish kingdom. In fact, during his third expedition Columbus was arrested and sent back to Spain in leg irons and chains.

The king and queen of Spain never really trusted Columbus and believed that he was carving out an empire for himself in the Americas. Although they did not sanction Columbus' arrest and deportation from the lands that he had discovered, his detainment was indicative of the Spanish crown's insecurity and controlling tendencies.

It needs to be remembered also that in 1492, the same year Columbus stumbled upon the New World, the Spanish royal family successfully regained full control of their country after the last Moorish kingdom of Granada surrendered. The Spanish crown read the capitulation of the Muslim king Abu Abdullah as providential and vowed that it would never again allow foreigners or those 'not of the faith' to settle on Spanish soil, including all Spanish territories such as those in the Americas. Columbus, although a good Catholic, was nonetheless a foreigner who ultimately 'could not be trusted'.

By the time of his death in 1506, Columbus was a peripheral figure in Spanish plans for a rapidly increasing American empire. It is reputed that Columbus went to his grave still convinced he had discovered the 'Indies' that were spoken about by Marco Polo on his journeys to the East. It is perhaps apt that very little in the current Americas bears Columbus' name. The Americas were allegedly named after his fellow countryman and explorer Amerigo Vespucci, while Columbus has to settle for the public holiday Columbus Day in the United States and the South American country Colombia.

By the early sixteenth century, the Iberian Peninsula (Spain and Portugal) controlled most of what was then the known world with Spain consolidating her grasp on the mainland territories and islands of the Americas, and Portugal strengthening her control of West Africa. The neighbours were maritime powers, totally focused on exploration and capturing lands for their kings and the kingdom of God, leading to a constant rivalry between the two countries. It is likely that they would have clashed at some point over ownership of overseas territories but religion intervened in the form of the pope. His

Holiness, Alexander VI, the Spanish-born pope, had no desire to witness two Catholic countries fighting for control of overseas provinces and implemented a papal bull, which would eventually become the Treaty of Tordesillas. This treaty split the known world into two with Spain taking everything west of the Azores, the islands in the Atlantic, and Portugal everything to the east. However, by some quirk of geography, Portugal managed to acquire the important South American country of Brazil.

Armed with the treaty, Spain then set about establishing an empire based around order and discipline – Spanish style. Interestingly, Queen Isabella was never in favour of slavery and put an end to Columbus' ideas of expanding the indigenous slave trade from the Americas to Europe. Unfortunately for the indigenous people, Queen Isabella's death in 1504 robbed them of their limited protection and gave a green light to those who placed no value on indigenous life.

Much has been said about the cruelty of the Spanish towards the indigenous people during their conquest of the Americas. The Spanish arrival brought a clash of civilizations, which pitted a medieval European country against the indigenous peoples of the West. The Spanish conquistador Bernal Diaz del Castillo, who accompanied Hernán Cortés on his conquest of Mexico in 1518, provides chilling eyewitness accounts of the range of Spanish abuses among the hapless indigenous people, especially during the 'pacification' of Mexico. His diaries capture the type of violence carried out, which witnessed indigenous people killed for target practice, out of boredom or to display human strength. Others perished from overwork in the silver and gold mines or on enclosure farms, and the Spanish also deployed forced labour to build their fortresses and towns.

However, the greatest devastation to the indigenous people was caused by animals and diseases. Like any colonizing nation, the Spanish transplanted various aspects of their culture into an alien environment but with mixed results. The animals they brought to supplement their diet proved detrimental to the indigenous people with goats, sheep, pigs and cattle eating their crops and foodstuffs. This resulted in malnutrition and, eventually, starvation. The Spanish also brought with them a range of communicable diseases against which the indigenous people had no resistance and, in the words of Columbus, they 'dropped like flies'.

It would be wrong to suggest that indigenous people all rolled over and died during the conquest of their countries. Like the Africans who would arrive a generation later, many indigenous people resisted the stringent demands of their new masters. In the Caribbean, where the Spanish had established their first bases, it would appear that war and cruelty held the upper hand over peace and generosity. By 1492, the two main indigenous groups in the region were the Arawaks and the Caribs. The historian Franklin W. Knight suggests that Arawaks were forced to flee between the various Caribbean landmasses because the Caribs were constantly raiding their territories and villages in search of women to replenish their communities.

Columbus first encountered the Arawaks when he arrived on a Bahamian island in 1492 and quickly assessed that they were peaceful people who would make good slaves. The Arawaks were by all accounts relatively peaceful folk who preferred social pursuits to anything warlike. Led by a *cacique* or chief, Arawaks preferred communal living and relaxation to invasion or fighting. Nonetheless, studies show that the Spanish rewarded their good nature with unparalleled cruelty and exploitation, decimating their numbers.

However, some Arawaks did shirk their general peaceful demeanour and fought the Spanish invaders in Hispaniola and

Cuba, but their efforts were often in vain because their spears and other homemade weapons were no match for Spanish armour and armaments. Others preferred flight to fight and fled to the hills in islands such as Jamaica, Cuba and Hispaniola where they established communities that lived in opposition to the Spanish. These communities would provide early inspiration for other groups who rebelled against the tyranny of certain aspects of European rule in the Americas.

Conversely, Columbus described the Caribs as stubborn, wild, ignorant and cannibalistic, mainly because they refused to accede to Spanish demands. Unlike the Arawaks, the Caribs were openly hostile to Columbus and his cohorts from the outset and fought against them when they arrived on their Caribbean islands. The Caribs used their superior knowledge of the terrain as well as sheer belligerence to create real problems for the Spanish on the smaller Caribbean islands, and this was one of the reasons why the Spanish preferred the larger Caribbean islands inhabited by the Arawaks. The irony is, however, that there are still sizeable Carib communities living on the Caribbean islands of Dominica, St Lucia and St Vincent – the term 'Caribbean' is derived from the word Carib – while the Arawaks have been completely wiped out. The only evidence of their existence today is found in names such as Jamaica (a derivative of the Arawak name Xaymaca) and artefacts found in various national museums.

It would be wrong to suggest that the Spanish did nothing to curb the excesses of their countrymen. When the Spanish crown became fully aware of the abuses inflicted upon the indigenous people, it appointed 'Indian' protectors to rein in the worst offenders. These protectors also had the responsibility of ensuring that the indigenous people were treated differently and exposed to good Christian teaching.

The first of the protectors was the Dominican friar, Montesinos, whose sermons demanded better moral behaviour on the part of the Spaniards, and condemned slavery, which he regarded as evil. His work in the Spanish West Indies resulted in the Spanish king drawing up the *Laws of Burgos* which acknowledged the right of Spaniards to use forced labour, but demanded that they treat the 'Indians' fairly and called on them to convert their charges by peaceful means. Friar Montesinos did his best under the circumstances and, in many respects, was the trailblazer for those who would later take up the 'Indian cause', such as Bartolomé de Las Casas.

Las Casas, a Spanish-born Dominican friar, has been described as the 'saviour of the Indians'. Like most of his countrymen before him, Las Casas had gone to the Americas as a young man to make his fortune and had little interest in the plight of the native people. However, his ordination as a priest resulted in a change of heart on the issue of indigenous slavery, and led to his first-rate work among the Indians and his reputation as protector. Las Casas petitioned the Spanish crown on behalf of the indigenous people, denounced indigenous slavery as cruel and immoral and argued that free labour would be more productive. Through this, he was given dispensation to engage in certain social experiments to prove that Indians had the capacity both to be good Christians and to work productively as free labourers.

In many respects, Las Casas' work mirrors that of the eighteenth-century British slave trade abolitionists, people such as Thomas Clarkson who would promote similar theories with regard to Africa and the slave trade. Las Casas' tireless efforts were chronicled in his infamous *History of the Indies*, a work noted for giving birth to the 'Black Legend' – stories recording the brutal excesses of his countrymen in the Americas during the birth of colonization.

However, from a Transatlantic Slave Trade perspective, Las Casas' real legacy was the sanction he gave to the Spanish crown for the mass importation of enslaved Africans to the Americas. The good friar was so concerned about the dwindling numbers of indigenous people that he petitioned the Spanish crown for Africans to be used as replacements.

The final entries in his journals reveal a priest tortured by his inability to do anything to help the Africans who were enduring the same abuses suffered by his beloved indigenous people. Las Casas died an old man who went to his grave regretting his decision to endorse African slavery. But at least he was spared the ultimate cruelty of seeing the total decimation of the Arawaks in Jamaica and Hispaniola.* Within a few generations of his death, they too would be confined to the history books as casualties of Spanish colonization in the Americas.

When he received Las Casas' initial request for African labour, the Spanish king had few qualms about using them as slaves as long as it bore dividends for the crown. The Spanish were familiar both with slavery as an institution and with Africans as slaves long before they arrived in the Americas, and they had drawn up laws to regulate and protect slaves living on Spanish soil as early as the thirteenth century. These regulations were part of the *Las Siete Partidas* (Seven Divisions), which were known to most Spaniards by the time the king received Las Casas' petition.

Similarly, the Portuguese exploration of Africa in the fifteenth century had introduced a fresh wave of Africans to the Iberian Peninsular. The Spanish regularly frequented Portuguese slaving markets in search of Christianized Africans whom they

---

* According to the historian Franklin W. Knight, the Arawak population on the island of Hispaniola numbered around 500,000. Within a few generations their numbers had been decimated.

used as slaves to carry out domestic duties in Spain and, more importantly, to cultivate sugar cane on the Canary Islands. Spain would later transplant this system of sugar production to the West Indies and the historian Eric Williams has suggested that by the time of his second voyage, Columbus had already decided that the region was ripe for sugar cultivation.

As a result, the first Africans brought to the Americas came from Spain and its colonies rather than Africa. These Africans fitted the bill for a number of reasons. They spoke Spanish, were familiar with the work they had to do and, most importantly, were Christians. The Spanish crown displayed what is now termed 'religious intolerance' in its attitude towards its American protectorates. The king and queen had previously decreed that 'no Moors, Jews or unbelievers' could enter their American territories. The New World would only be populated by 'good Christians' which meant that only baptized Africans could be transported to the Americas, such as those sent from Spain to Hispaniola in 1505 to replace the indigenous people grafting in the country's mines.

By 1510, the king gave orders for 50 more enslaved Africans to be 'sent to the Indies'. But the Transatlantic Slave Trade was truly initiated in 1517 when the king issued the first contact or *asiento* to supply Spain with a regular number of Africans per annum for a fixed number of years. The *asiento* was a licence to print money, and for the next three centuries various European countries would fight Portugal for the right to supply Spain with enslaved Africans for its growing American empire.

But what of the Africans who were sent to carry out the work previously done by indigenous people? Despite Las Casas' assertion that Africans were built of sturdier stuff than indigenous people, they still died in significant numbers and from the same causes as their indigenous counterparts. The major contrast between the sufferings of the two was that Africans did not have their equivalent of Las Casas in the sixteenth century, and had to wait almost two centuries before voices from church and society were raised in their favour. Additionally, the supply of African labour appeared limitless in European eyes; no sooner did one die than another could easily be obtained as a replacement. And it was this seemingly inexhaustible nature of the labour pool that acted as one of the central reasons for African enslavement.

There is little doubt that the Spanish crown turned to Africans because it could not find sufficient numbers of its countrymen to carry out this exploitative labour. From the outset of colonization, Spain was eager to reproduce its way of life throughout the Americas and was aware that it needed fellow citizens to achieve this. Nevertheless, nation building was hard work and it needed a skilled, flexible workforce to carry out roles such as administrators, clerks and craftsmen. But before these individuals could begin their important work, basic labourers were required to clear land, plant crops and construct buildings. This was onerous work, especially in the hot, disease-infested regions of the Americas.

The Spanish crown quickly discovered that far too many of their citizens had no desire to carry out work that they deemed beneath them. Most Spaniards, like other Europeans who would follow, went to the Americas to seek their fortunes in the gold and silver mines rather than to work as labourers. The Americas were regarded as lands where precious metals oozed from the earth; they were also the home of *El Dorado* (the Gilded One or the golden man), who symbolized the fertility of the region. It was hard, therefore, to convince Spaniards to work as farmers or labourers for meagre wages when the colonies had the potential to enrich the daring, hardworking explorer. Furthermore, many whites wanted to work for themselves rather than an employer, with the ideal scenario involving a purchase of land on which they would earn enough money to support their families.

It has often been suggested that white men and women did not have the resources to carry out hard work in hot, energy-sapping conditions. This theory must be questioned, however, because many of the first Spaniards came from southern Spain or the Canary Islands where the temperatures are similar at certain times of the year to those found in the Americas. No such question was asked in those regions about their capacity to work hard in the hot sun. And yet in his seminal but controversial book, *Capitalism and Slavery*, Eric Williams argued that ethnic difference was a minor factor in the choice of slaves and these racial stereotypes only became an issue much later on in the history of slavery. Williams suggests that Europeans were desperate for labourers and would have 'gone to the moon, if necessary, for labour. Africa though was nearer than the moon and also nearer than the more populous countries of India and China'.[3]

White labour failed to take hold in the Americas for a number of reasons. In the Caribbean islands such as Barbados and Antigua, white peasants found it impossible to compete with large landowners for land, and land became a premium in such regions due to the emergence of sugar and other cash crops. In fact, sugar proved to be the proverbial flame that drew the African moth to its ruin – it was considered the 'oil' of its day in the West. But sugar production was labour intensive and required a lot of land in order to yield appropriate returns. Plantations or factories where sugar was produced needed further labourers to do everything from planting the crop during the season to cutting the cane during harvest. Plantations also required labourers to use the machinery to extract the juice from the cane, and to turn that juice into molasses and sugar. Further workers were employed as carpenters, smiths and coopers to maintain the equipment on the plantation.

Planters soon realized that the bigger the plantation, the more sugar they could produce, although increased productivity obviously required more Africans. On smaller territories and islands, planters quickly seized the land, leaving little opportunity for white peasant farmers to eke out an existence. In fact, in the early days of English settlement in the West Indies, a sizeable number of white farmers grew tobacco in St Kitts and Barbados. However, the arrival of sugar as the dominant crop, the escalation of large plantations and the beginning of slave labour saw many abandon tobacco and leave the smaller islands in favour of mainland America or the larger Caribbean islands, as they could not cope with the demands of slave labour with its need for land.

Although sugar production quickly became synonymous with slavery, the sugar industry was initially very dependent on white indentured labour from Europe. England first began to make inroads into Spanish territory in the 1620s, on islands such as Barbados and St Kitts. According to the historian Gad Heuman,[4] St Kitts was the first permanent non-Spanish colony in the region, and in 1624, French and English settlers shared the island in a defensive alliance against Spanish attacks. Three years later, another group of English colonists established a colony on Barbados.

But first under Columbus, and then under other explorers, Spain had mapped and settled most of the New World by the early sixteenth century. However, it preferred to concentrate on the bigger West Indian islands as well as the mainland, as countless Spanish kings believed that larger territories provided greater opportunities for settlement and precious metal reserves, ensuring that the smaller West Indian islands lay neglected. England and France soon became aware of this through the activities of pirates, privateers and buccaneers who regularly sacked the Spanish ships of their booty between the Americas and Spain. Many of these pirates had headquarters on poorly guarded or unoccupied islands – territories ripe for conquest – and the 1620s would become the era when England obtained a toehold in the West Indies. This would later become a stranglehold, encompassing well over 60 per cent of the ownership of West Indian islands.

England soon encountered the problems faced by Spain, which included fighting off interlopers and developing the necessary infrastructure for settlement and colonization. But unlike the Spanish, diseases, famine and sustained cruelty had depopulated the indigenous population to such an extent that the English could not rely on their labour to assist her in this important activity in the West Indies. Indigenous labour was only a significant factor in the American state of Virginia.

England and France initially looked to their own shores to fill the labour gap, settling on white indentured labour rather than slavery in order to resolve shortages. Workers signed a contract to work for an agreed time (usually five to seven years) in return for their passage. Unlike Spain, which still had both slavery and slave laws on its native soil, England had long abandoned slavery for serfdom and contracted labour was more in keeping with the latter. But it also found other ways of populating the new colonies, which included sending its convicts to the West Indies on a one-way ticket. In time, this policy was extended to peasants, prostitutes, petty criminals and others who were an eyesore or a cost to the public purse.

England would subsequently use this policy as an alternative punishment for those who broke its draconian penal regulations. Men, women and children who broke the law for vagrancy, begging or petty larceny were offered Hobson's Choice – either a one-way trip to the West Indies or the gallows. As a consequence, in the seventeenth century the West Indies turned from a land of opportunity for adventurers, entrepreneurs and those fleeing persecution into a dumping ground for some of Europe's most undesirable characters.

Long before Bristol gained a reputation as a leading British slaving port, the city was the centre of the country's indentured labour industry with tens of thousands of people leaving the seaport on route to the West Indies. It was the last sight many men, women and children would have of their beloved country as they headed for new lives in the West Indies. Some would return after their five or ten-year stints on the plantations or farms, while others remained to eke out an existence in countries such as Barbados, where they earned the rather derogatory name of 'redlegs', which described the effects of the tropical sun on their fair-skinned legs.

Although English, Scottish and Irish labourers were sent in their thousands to the West Indies, such was the insatiable appetite of the sugar industry for labourers that these numbers would never be enough. The need for more workers resulted in various underhand means to obtain labour, and in the second half of the seventeenth century, kidnapping flourished in port cities such as Bristol and London. Abduction took various forms from the straightforward snatch-and-grab approach to the more subtle application of plying an unfortunate individual with strong liquor. The latter would then invariably wake up the next morning – literally all at sea – nursing a hangover and the realization that they would be spending the next few years in the West Indies.

Additionally, sea captains with investments in the West Indies were not averse to visiting inns or brothels armed with travellers' tales of tremendous wealth and opportunity to entice naive, gullible or impressionable young men and women. Those who were down on their luck or fleeing debtors did not need a captain's sweet words to convince them and signed on the dotted line before he could say 'West Indies'.

However, a captain's fanciful descriptions of the 'Indies' in some dingy tavern in Bristol bore no resemblance to the daily reality of life for most whites in the West Indies. The West Indies in the seventeenth century was nothing like the beautiful, idyllic landscapes and white sandy beaches that entice sun-seekers from around the globe today. The white labourers who turned bronze did so on plantations rather than beaches, as they dug, hoed and planted sugar, potatoes and other crops in the scorching sun. Anyone who could not keep pace was whipped or flogged as planters strived to get the last ounce of labour from them. Because they were in their service for a limited time, it was in their employers' best interests to extract as much work out of them as possible. As a result, many never lived to see the end of their contract, while others were so worn out by the end of their tenure that they could not work again.

It would be tempting to argue that indentured servitude was little more than slavery in another guise and that the white labourers suffered as much as enslaved Africans. However, this is far from the truth. Contracted labour did not seek to reduce the European to the status of an animal and, unlike the mistreatment of Africans, there was no determined attempt to rob them of their names, religions or culture. Likewise, although indentured labourers were treated very badly during their contract, many held on to the hope that they would be free after a finite period of servitude, and where there is hope, there is life. Furthermore, any offspring born to them during indentureship were free and not condemned to slavery like Africans. Most importantly, the colour white was invariably associated with freedom while black was always connected to slavery, ensuring that free Africans always had to carry papers with them in order to prove their liberty.

Many white-indentured labourers absconded from estates or farms to live out their lives under an assumed name without arousing suspicion. Africans never had that luxury and Olaudah Equiano, in his seminal autobiography, mentions how Africans who had bought their freedom or held a 'free' paper were always in danger of being sold back into slavery, regardless of their free status.

He writes, 'There was a very clever and decent free young mulatto* man who sailed a long time with us: he had a free woman for his wife, by whom he had a child, and she was then living on shore and all very happy. Our captain and mate and other people on board... all knew this young man... It happened that a Bermudas captain whose vessel lay here for a few days in the road came aboard of us and seeing the mulatto man, whose name was Joseph Clipson, he told him he was not free and that he had orders from his master to bring him to Bermudas... Although he showed a certificate of his being born free in St Kitt's... yet he was taken forcibly out of our vessel... and the next day, without giving the poor man any hearing on shore or suffering him even to see his wife or child, he was carried away and probably doomed never more to see them again.'[5]

---

* 'Mulatto' was a pejorative term for the offspring, usually, of a white male and African female, and the word is a derivation of 'mule' – the sterile progeny of a horse and donkey.

3

African Chattel Enslavement

The one who invents is not always the one who benefits the most, and so it was with the Transatlantic Slave Trade. The Portuguese were the first to initiate the trade, but England was the country to reap the most benefits from it. It was during the reign of Queen Elizabeth I that England first entered the murky waters of slave trading – a full 100 years after the Portuguese. But by the eighteenth century, Britain would perfect the trade and become one of the world's leading slave-trading nations.

Sir John Hawkins, the Plymouth-born merchant, is chiefly credited as the first Englishman to successfully trade in Africans. Depending on your viewpoint, Hawkins was an adventurer, an entrepreneur, a pirate or a brigand. What is not beyond debate is that in 1562, Hawkins led an expedition-cum-raiding-party to what is now Sierra Leone and seized around 300 Africans. Hawkins' escapades were important because they were one of the first real attempts to break the then Portuguese monopoly on the slave trade that was servicing Spain's ever-increasing need for labour.

Ironically, as England did not possess any colonies in the Americas during the sixteenth century, Hawkins' slave-trading efforts primarily involved selling Africans to the ever-grateful Spanish who controlled such territories, which meant that he was indirectly aiding the country that Britain would fight just a couple of decades later.

Although Hawkins gained notoriety for introducing England to the slave trade, English trading with Africa can be traced back to 1553, when Captain Thomas Windham, acting under the auspices of London traders, led an expedition of 140 people to the Guinea Coast to search for gold. Unfortunately, Windham failed to heed the advice of his Portuguese guide (advising him against entering the 'Bite of Benin'), resulting in the death of 100 of the crew.

Undeterred by the Windham disaster, however, the following year John Lok (not to be confused with the English philosopher and slave-trading financial investor John Locke) led an expedition of three ships to the Guinea coast. The Lok-led adventure secured not only ivory and gold, but also a dozen Africans whom he brought back to England to amuse Elizabethan crowds. By all accounts, Queen Elizabeth I was unimpressed with his antics and commanded that he release the Africans. It needs to be noted that the queen was no campaigner against African exploitation; her attitude would mirror that of later generations who were content to make money out of human misery, as long as they did not have to confront the victims.

The Africans obtained by Hawkins during his slave raiding expeditions were exchanged on the north coast of the island of Hispaniola (modern-day Haiti and the Dominican Republic) and he returned to England with a full shipload of animal hides and sugar. This commerce between Europe, Africa and the Americas became known as the 'triangular trade' and Hawkins is again credited as the man who initiated this commerce between the continents. But although Hawkins applied for licences and paid the associated customs fees in order to buy and sell in the West Indies, he was still trading illegally, and this would rebound on him during a later trading adventure.

The role of the royal family in Hawkins' adventures makes for very interesting reading. Initially, Queen Elizabeth I was appalled at Hawkins' activities in Africa, but she changed her attitude when the trader presented her with a share of the booty. Hawkins subsequently informed the queen of the potential to make money from this lucrative enterprise, and for his second voyage in 1564, she provided Hawkins with the *Jesus of Lubeck*, a vessel built to destroy any seafaring opposition. Once again, Hawkins used kidnapping and violence rather than bartering to obtain 'human cargo' from the west coast of Africa.

His second adventure to Africa was far from smooth and he encountered difficulties from Africans on Sherbro Island off the south-western coast of Sierra Leone. They got wind of his activities and put up a fight against his snatch-and-grab escapades. This was probably one of the first recorded instances of African opposition to English slave trading but it would certainly not be the last.

It has been estimated that investors in Hawkins' ventures had a 60 per cent return on their investments. One of these was probably Queen Elizabeth I because she rewarded Hawkins with a knighthood. It needs to be pointed out that history does not record whether the queen or other investors were fully aware of the true nature of Hawkins' activities in Africa and there is evidence to suggest that he was economical with the truth about what constituted 'trade' and 'cargo' from Africa.

The now titled Hawkins set out on his third African adventure in 1567 and one of his crew members was his cousin, Francis Drake, who would also receive a knighthood for battling the Spanish in 1588. However, 20 years before this Spanish skirmish, Drake was helping Hawkins in his search for Africans. Hawkins' third and final expedition was not as financially rewarding as the previous ones. He failed to secure his desired number of slaves due to African resistance, while the Spanish – now aware of his interloping throughout the Spanish Main – instituted a crackdown. Not only did Hawkins find it difficult to sell his enslaved Africans in the West Indies, but he also came under fire from Spanish galleons. Indeed the Spanish gave him a good hiding and sent him limping home minus many of his ships. Still, he had become something of a hero in England, and armed with a king's (or should that be a queen's) ransom of money, he became very wealthy with his own coat of arms to boot. Hawkins ended his years as a treasurer to the queen's navy.

For a man who was so celebrated during his time, there is very little today dedicated to his memory. Although his hometown of Plymouth has his coat of arms displayed on the west side of the Victorian Armada Memorial and a Sir John Hawkins Square tucked away in a corner of the city centre, there is little doubt that he remains a poor second to his venerated kinsman and fellow seaman, Sir Francis Drake.

Drake has a statue on Plymouth Hoe, the large public space looking out onto the seafront that provides views to Drake's Island and the Plymouth Sound. There are other frequent reminders of Drake around Plymouth and male tour guides often dress in Drake-like costumes to show sightseers around the coastal port. The irony is that Drake was not even born in Plymouth, but in nearby Tavistock. It would appear that his involvement in slave trading in Africa and privateering (legalized piracy) on the Spanish Main have been redeemed by his naval antics against the Spanish Armada. In today's highly critical world, Hawkins has fewer redeeming qualities.

The real legacy of Hawkins' three triangular trade voyages was arguably the normalization of African slave trading among the English. It is important to note that during the sixteenth century, England was unfamiliar with institutionalized slavery. Unlike her main European slave-trading rivals, Portugal and Spain, who had existing laws governing the treatment of enslaved Africans, England turned her back on slavery after the Normans had established themselves in the country. England preferred serfdom and other forms of controlled labour to slavery, and as a consequence, Hawkins' departure into slavery went very much against the English belief in liberty and justice – as enshrined in the Magna Carta.

The English adventurer and author Richard Jobson echoed this belief in English freedom and justice; when offered enslaved Africans in the early part of the sixteenth century, he retorted, 'We are people who do not deal in such commodities.' Jobson went on to suggest that those Englishmen partaking in such activity had dubious reputations and were little better than their slave-trading Portuguese, Spanish and Dutch counterparts.

Although slave trading was regarded as an unsuitable profession for an Englishman, it was an obvious moneymaking venture. England looked on in envy as the Portuguese appeared to be making a small fortune supplying Spain with enslaved Africans for her ever-expanding American territories. The temptation proved too much for Queen Elizabeth I and in 1588, the year of the Armada, she granted ten-year rights to London merchants to trade exclusively on the West African coast. Interestingly, these merchants ignored the lucrative trade in human beings and sought more legitimate commerce with those living along the African shorelines.

Why the English failed to enter the slave trade at this time is a matter for some discussion. Some have argued that apart from the unscrupulous activities of adventurers like Hawkins, most of the English people, as Jobson asserted, were above such criminal deeds. However, a careful reading of the history of the time would suggest that England's lack of interest in slave trading had more to do with pragmatism than with altruism. England had no colonies of her own in the Americas until the seventeenth century, so any slave trading involved commerce with its European rivals. For example, Hawkins offloaded his enslaved Africans to the Spanish who would later use the monies accrued from its territories in the Americas to battle with the English during the Armada.

The reality was that when England gained ownership of islands in the West Indies, it soon became all systems go with regard to slave trading and any of the qualms mentioned by Jobson and others were ignored in the pursuit of profits. In time, the slave trade would become respectable for most English people and Africans would be considered 'sub-human' cargo, to be readily traded and exchanged for other valuable commodities.

Although the English would become one of the prime movers in the Transatlantic Slave Trade, the Portuguese had been trafficking Africans since 1444. According to one historian, the Portuguese 'thought it the most natural thing to seize the first group of Africans they saw and carry them away to Lisbon as gifts for prominent ladies and gentlemen'.[1] By 1482, they were so involved in the slave trade that the Portuguese king, Manuel I, ordered the construction of the infamous Elmina castle fort in what is now Ghana. Elmina or *El Mina* (meaning 'the mine' in Portuguese) acquired its name from Portuguese adventurers who believed the area had an abundance of gold mines.

Gold was also the reason why the English renamed the area the 'Gold Coast', and West African gold and English fortunes would come to fruition in the seventeenth century during the reign of Charles II. In 1663, England issued the guinea coin which was the equivalent to 20 shillings or a pound. Most of the first coins were minted from gold that came from the Guinea Coast – the Gold Coast, Senegal, Gambia and Guinea. The gold was brought to Britain by the Royal Africa Company (RAC), the trading company established by Charles II to exploit Africa's natural resources. Portugal had stationed its naval and military forces at Elmina to repel all would-be interlopers, while inside the notorious stronghold enslaved Africans were held captive in its almost impregnable warehouses along with the gold that was stored there.

Elmina was one of many slave fortresses or castles that lined the coast of West Africa during the seventeenth century. The Portuguese would use these bases as the headquarters of both their slave-trading activities and all other business they had on the continent at that time. These slave forts, many of which are still standing today and are reminiscent of the castles found on the west coast of Wales, were often the last structures Africans saw during their forced departure from their homeland.

However, before leaving their countries, the Portuguese insisted that they were branded and baptized as 'good Catholics'. Portugal, just like Spain, believed it was the Christian duty of every man to 'convert the heathen'. As a result, Portuguese priests took their conversion responsibilities very seriously in Africa, especially when given the incentive of receiving a fee for every African baptized.

One of the great arguments or areas of debate surrounding European slave trading was the fact that, prior to the arrival of the white people, indigenous slavery and a slave trade had already existed in Africa for centuries. Historians such as Ronald Segal and Humphrey J. Fisher argue that Arab traders were largely responsible for introducing the concept of slave trading on the continent, and point to the fact that the Arab or Trans-Saharan Slave Trade predated its Transatlantic counterpart by at least seven centuries and matched it for numbers in terms of people trafficked.[2] For the most part, the Trans-Saharan Slave Trade involved the overland movement of Africans from West and Central Africa to the Middle East and beyond, as well as sea routes from East Africa through the Red Sea and Indian Ocean.

There were clear similarities between the Trans-Saharan and Transatlantic Slave Trades. Both used coercion and deception to take Africans from their homeland and religion was a central feature of this approach. However, the traditional belief is that Arab slavery was more humane than the Transatlantic Slave Trade because 'the values and attitudes promoted by religion inhibited the very development of a Western-style capitalism, with its effective subjugation of people to the priority profit'.[3] But while Arab slavery appeared not to have the brutal characteristics of its European counterpart, there was still a clear racial dimension to the enslavement of Africans, with physical and psychological abuse taking place and enslaved Africans' rights often being violated.

The traditional view of Arab slavery is that it largely involved non-Muslims. In other words, infidels or unbelievers were primary targets for enslavement. Similarly, it was argued that infidels embracing Islam were immediately freed, although there is clear evidence that African Muslims were also targets for enslavement and that conversion was not a means to emancipation.

As well as the Trans-Saharan Slave Trade, Africa also had its own form of slavery that had been taking place on the continent for several centuries and was one of the factors that Europe was able to exploit when it instigated the Transatlantic Slave Trade. Olaudah Equiano, the former enslaved African who became a leading abolitionist, suggested that prior to his capture in West Africa his father had 'many slaves' and that slavery as an institution was common in his part of the world. In African society, men and women were enslaved for criminal behaviour, adultery, war or debt. In many parts of the continent, imprisonment for criminal activities was an unfamiliar concept and slavery served as both a deterrent and a punishment. In his autobiography, Equiano mentions that enslaved Africans were given to a wronged party as compensation, and that adultery was punished by enslavement. Africans also made slaves of those captured in wars between rival kingdoms and clans, and it was this particular method of enslavement that grew during the Transatlantic Slave Trade and which is still the subject of much debate.

In certain African kingdoms, autocrats governed their subjects with an iron fist and owned enslaved Africans in order to exhibit their potency. Other Africans possessed them to display their affluence, but it would appear that most were kept for domestic purposes. For example, during crop time it was not unusual for farmers to acquire enslaved Africans to tackle the increased workloads, and the wealthy relied on this form of labour to carry out a variety of household chores.

Today, all slavery is regarded as a human rights violation and roundly condemned by most 'civilized' societies – modern society takes a dim view of one person owning another as this invariably results in exploitation and abuse. There is little doubt that the Transatlantic Slave Trade helped to characterize this common understanding of slavery which reduces human beings to possessions or property. Many African scholars in particular are keen to distinguish indigenous slavery from the chattel enslavement that we associate with the Americas from the sixteenth to the nineteenth centuries. Likewise, they are eager to draw attention both to the reasons for and the effects of the Transatlantic Slave Trade.

If one looks at the issue of indigenous slavery, it is possible to argue that it was not characterized by the cruelty, dehumanization and human rights violations of later chattel enslavement. Although it is important not to view what took place through rose-tinted spectacles or use words such as 'benign' or 'benevolent' to describe indigenous slavery, it did afford enslaved Africans greater latitude, respect and social mobility. Most importantly, it treated them as human beings rather than mere commodities or possessions.

Indigenous African enslavement was often so complex that it blurred the lines between freedom and slavery. In many African societies, enslaved Africans were treated reasonably by their owners and were allowed to keep their names, practise their religions and hold on to many aspects of their culture. Some African societies welcomed the cultural enrichment and life skills of their enslaved Africans and it was not uncommon for them to marry into their host's family and lose their slave status. A further incongruous feature was the possibility of enslaved Africans owning property and even other slaves. This occurred in several kingdoms known for giving enslaved Africans much leeway.

Indigenous slavery was often very dynamic and allowed the potential for social mobility through aptitude or skill. It was possible for enslaved Africans to become kings or great leaders in African societies; such was the case of King JaJa of Opobo or Kauran Chachi of Abuja (both in modern-day Nigeria). In the late seventeenth century, Anterashi, a slave of the Sultan of Bornu (in modern-day Chad) was made the Commander in Chief of the Bornu army and warden of the southern section of the Bornu empire, and there are other instances of captured warriors holding down positions of authority within the king's courts.

Africans often encouraged their slaves to marry and raise families. Moreover, the children of such relationships were not routinely considered to be enslaved Africans. In such societies, they often took advantage of manumission laws (laws pertaining to the freedom of enslaved Africans) to become free individuals and, ironically, purchase slaves themselves to reinforce their status as free persons.

Although indigenous slavery was an intricate facet of African culture, Africans societies did not appear dependent on it for their survival. Conversely, the chattel enslavement that characterized the Americas was based on terror and violence. Academics such as Orlando Patterson point out the covert dehumanizing process of chattel enslavement which sought to strip Africans of their cultural practices and instilled subservience. Additionally, Africans had very few rights in the West: their children were normally considered enslaved Africans and were also subject to the same abuses as them. There was little opportunity for social mobility and freedom and any notion of marriage with a member of their master's family was unthinkable.

The issue of the impact of the Transatlantic Slave Trade on African society, which we looked at briefly in the first chapter, has also been the subject of great debate. This largely centres around African culpability in the Transatlantic Slave Trade and the question of whether Africa benefited from its interaction with Europe over the human trade. There is little doubt that it would be inappropriate to use terms such as 'Africans sold Africans' because this serves as a way of absolving Europe from any guilt in the slave trade. And yet there was a clear African dimension to what took place over the 400 years of its duration, with Africans primarily going on slave raiding expeditions in order to obtain enslaved Africans for Europeans.

One of the best known songs of the late great Jamaican musical maestro Bob Marley, 'Redemption Song', starts with the words, 'Pirates, yes, they rob I, and sold I to the merchants' ships'. These lyrics allude to the slave trade and there is little doubt in Marley's mind that the 'pirates' or slave traders were white. And yet studies reveal that these pirates were helped by Africans who carried out the physical 'robbing', taking the enslaved people to the 'merchants' ships'.

During the early years of the Transatlantic Slave Trade, Africans enslaved those living in or near the coastal regions; however, increased competition between slave-procuring clans on the coast led many Africans to turn their attention to the vast interior regions. These slave raiding ventures would often involve a trek of hundreds of miles in search of slaves. Equiano gives a graphic description of his own capture: 'One day, when all our people were gone out to their works as usual and only I and my sister were left to mind the house, two men and a woman got over our walls, and in a moment seized us both, and without giving us time to cry out or make resistance, stopped our mouths, and ran off with us into the nearest woods. Here they tied our hands and continued to carry us as far as they could till night came on…'.[4]

In his account of the abolition of the slave trade, one of the leading abolitionists, Thomas Clarkson, describes a slave raid. 'They concealed themselves under the bushes. In this position they remained during daylight. But at night they went to [the village] armed, and seized all the inhabitants, who had not time to make their escape. They obtained 45 persons in this manner.'[5]

Once the slave raiding parties found their unfortunate quarry, the newly enslaved Africans faced an excruciating march to the coast in shackles, coffles and other restraints. This walk could take months and substantial numbers succumbed to malnutrition, disease and ill-treatment. Slave raiders, however, had few cares for those who fell ill on the journey or could not keep pace and killed anyone who slowed their return to the coast. Once there, the deal was completed with the agent who would sometimes brand the enslaved Africans with the names of their new owners and house them in barracoons or holding cells, to await transfer to the slaver (slave ship).

Barracoons were little more than dimly-lit dungeons whose cramped, air-starved conditions accounted for the deaths of many of those already weakened by the long trek. The favoured location for a barracoon was an island just off the coast from which it was hard for enslaved Africans to escape and which a rescue party would find it difficult to reach. Africans were housed in such conditions until the merchant had the required number to be loaded onto the slaver. John Newton's journals are a good indication of the lengthiness of the process involved in obtaining a shipload of enslaved Africans. His slaver that had arrived at the Guinea Coast one December was still moored there the following spring.

It has often been argued that the Transatlantic Slave Trade thrived because Africans assisted the Europeans in capturing and exchanging slaves. Quobna Ottobah Cugoano, the former enslaved African turned abolitionist, posed the hypothetical suggestion, 'had there been no buyers, there would have been no sellers'.[6] Unfortunately for Cugoano and the millions of others who were forced into slavery, Europeans were clearly interested in slave labour, and Africans of different religions, ethnic groupings and kingdoms participated in meeting their needs.

It is a clear misconception to suggest that Europeans used the snatch-and-grab tactics of Sir John Hawkins to obtain their slaves. By the seventeenth century, Europeans had slave forts littering the coastal areas of West Africa, forts that became the centres of the slave trade. It was here that European agents arranged meetings with numerous African kings and chiefs to negotiate prices and agree on numbers for slaves.

In the sixteenth and seventeenth centuries, there was little by the way of an international currency so an alternative means of bartering became the main means of negotiation. The system of exchange varied at different times and in different places, and in some parts of West Africa human beings were exchanged for weapons and alcohol. In other parts, cowrie shells from the Indian Ocean islands were the currency of choice. Additionally, as the Jamaican historian Richard Hart points out, certain West African kingdoms with an interest in metal work preferred iron bars, brass kettles and pans. It would be untrue to suggest that Europeans bartered worthless objects to gullible African kings in return for enslaved labourers. There is evidence that African rulers knew exactly what they wanted from these exchanges, and would readily turn on white traders if they thought they were being deceived. And while it was not unknown for an Africa ruler to leave these financial encounters ludicrously bedecked in trinkets, overcoats and powdered wigs, they also departed with weapons that would tighten their grip over rival kingdoms who were also trying to control the slave trade.

European weapons enabled West African kingdoms such as Dahomey (modern-day Benin) and Oyo (modern-day Nigeria) to become hubs of the slave trade and their rulers used an assortment of English firearms to attack neighbouring kingdoms in order to enslave their people. Ironically, studies show that some of the most vocal opponents of William Wilberforce's parliamentary work to end slave trading were West African kings. These rulers were regularly informed by European slave traders of the progress – or the lack of it – of the abolitionist campaigns in Britain, but when the Abolition Bill became law in 1807, some of the African kings physically wept at the thought of their lucrative businesses coming to an end. Certain rulers even considered petitioning King George III to reinstate British slave trading.

While it is true that some rulers exchanged enslaved people with Europeans without any care for their welfare, many others did not. Indeed, many directly opposed the slave trade, such as King Agaja of Dahomey (modern-day Benin), who during his reign in the mid 1720s abolished the slave trade in his kingdom and petitioned European countries to do likewise. Additionally, Nzinga Mbemba of the Congo wrote to the Portuguese crown in the sixteenth century stating his wish to end the slave trade in his country.

What also must be considered is that many African rulers participating in the slave trade may have believed that slavery in the Americas was similar to their indigenous version and were totally unaware of the violence and terror that awaited their countrymen in the Americas. This was especially the case as very few enslaved Africans were given the opportunity to return to their homelands with tales of the brutality of chattel slavery. Nevertheless, there is evidence that when many kings or rulers finally realized what was really taking place in the Americas they resisted the Europeans – often to no avail.

The complicity debate also needs to be looked at from another perspective as it can be argued that Europeans introduced the notion of African uniformity or homogeneity to the continent. According to Sylviane A. Diouf, 'Nowhere in the Africans' testimonies is there any indication that they felt betrayed by people "the color of their own skin". Their perspective was based on their worldview that recognized ethnic, political, and religious differences but not the modern concepts of a black race or African-ness. With time, when an encompassing African – no longer an ethnic – consciousness developed in America, the story passed on was not that people had been sold by other Africans but that they had been individually tricked and abducted by whites enticing them from the slave ships with European goods. For the most part these were not descriptions of actual events – although some certainly were – but allegorical tales that assigned blame where the Africans and their descendants thought it belonged: with the people who came to take them away... As has been evidenced elsewhere, the concepts of Africa, Africans, blackness, whiteness, and race did not exist in Africa, and they cannot be utilized today to assess people's actions at a time when they were not operative.' [7]

Diouf is also alluding to the fact that it is inappropriate to use such terms as complicity and 'selling each other' with regard to the slave trade because very few people would apply such logic to other internecine events. For instance, very few would describe the protracted 'troubles' in Northern Ireland as an intra-white issue. Instead, a more sophisticated and accurate description would be used that encompassed notions of religion, culture, identity and even ethnicity. But if one interprets the 'Irish' question using that framework, it would appear inconsistent and simplistic to suggest that 'Africans sold Africans' during the slave trade when Africa is not a country but the world's second-largest continent, with a huge diversity of religions, ethnicities and cultures.

The controversy over African 'collusion' in the Transatlantic Slave Trade is only matched by the debate over whether the prolonged trade in human beings stunted or developed Africa. The first point that is beyond any doubt is that Africa was undoubtedly the loser in its 'commercial' exchanges with Europe. The Transatlantic Slave Trade was a European invention – there is little evidence of Africans transporting enslaved people to the Americas prior to the arrival of

Europeans – and over several centuries, Europe obtained Africa's fittest, youngest and most capable men and women. Their labour, rather than being used to help develop their own countries, was employed in the Americas to assist in the production of goods that transformed the economies of European cities such as Nantes, Bristol, Liverpool and London. In return, Africa obtained European products such as cloths, iron, brass, beads and crockery which – depending on who you believe – either stunted the Africans' ability to develop these skills themselves or flooded their societies with items such as guns and brandy with disastrous effects.

According to the abolitionist MP, William Wilberforce, all manner of tactics were employed 'to encourage the chieftains to buy brandy and gun powder, to go to war and make slaves…'.[8.] Furthermore, John Newton, the slave trader turned Anglican preacher argued, 'I verily believe, that the far greater part of wars in Africa would cease, if the Europeans would cease to tempt them, by offering goods for slaves.'[9]

Wilberforce and Newton raised the controversial issue of the detrimental effect the Transatlantic Slave Trade was having on Africa. There is little doubt that both men were correct, for example, in suggesting that the emergence of the Transatlantic Slave Trade increased the number of wars on the continent. Traditionally, battles in many parts of Africa were fought for defensive purposes, such as to curtail the threat of a potential adversary. These conflicts invariably involved the selection of warriors or champions who fought a limited skirmish on behalf of their clans. The Transatlantic Slave Trade introduced a new dimension to wars with groups attacking old adversaries solely for the purpose of acquiring slaves to trade to Europeans. Consequently, slavery went from being a by-product of war or criminal behaviour into a major industry that many European traders instigated by deliberately supplying African kingdoms with arms to attack their rivals.

It can also be argued that the Transatlantic Slave Trade crippled traditional African industries. Many African societies quickly abandoned their customary activities such as weaving, wood and metal work, farming or fishing, for the more profitable work of capturing people for enslavement. A contemporary comparison might be the dubious narcotics trade, which involves farmers in poorer parts of the world deserting the cultivation of established crops for the more lucrative poppy, marijuana plant or cocoa leaf.

During the eighteenth century, at the height of the Transatlantic Slave Trade, the west coast of Africa was regarded as the white man's graveyard with many a slave trader succumbing to diseases such as small pox or yellow fever. But if disease did not threaten them, irate Africans did. Many Africans turned on the white slave traders for a number of reasons. Some Africans took exception to the presence of white interlopers and killed as many as they could get their hands on. Others, who had entered into negotiations with them, subsequently turned on their business partners if they believed they had been short-changed or robbed in their deals. It was not unknown for agents to be kidnapped by their African business associates if the latter felt they had been betrayed. Even when Africans were adequately recompensed, they often failed to release their captives.

When the French philosopher Voltaire claimed that 'history is just a portrayal of crimes and misfortunes', he was unwittingly describing the Middle Passage, the infamous Atlantic crossing of slavers from Africa to the Americas. Much has been written about this tragic, drawn-out episode in human history, and the figures involved have the potential to both amaze and disgust.

It has been estimated that between the sixteenth and nineteenth centuries, 9–12 million Africans were forcibly taken to the Americas for a life of slavery.[10] Other academics such as Herbert S. Klein put the figure at 10.25 million,[11] with David Eltis' figures also falling within this range. However, some historians such as Joseph E. Inikori have argued that this figure is nearer 15 million.[12] But whoever is right, this was – and still is – one of the largest known forced mass movements of human beings the world has ever witnessed.

It has been estimated that around 40 per cent of slave ships went to Brazil while the Caribbean took a similar number, the Spanish territories around 15 per cent and the United States the remainder. However, many of the Caribbean-bound Africans were subsequently shipped to North America, and this trans-shipment became so great that until the 1820s Africans outnumbered Europeans by a ratio of 5:1 throughout many parts of the Americas.

The figures quoted tell a disquieting story, yet statistics fail to fully convey the brutality and horror of the Transatlantic Slave Trade. It is far too easy these days to spend time arguing – as some are doing – over the exact amount of people transported, ships sailed or money made, and to forget, as many did centuries ago, that at the heart of the debate lay real human lives. Each ship that set sail from the African coast contained men, women and children who had been torn away from their loved ones. These individuals would never see their homelands again; indeed, many would never arrive at their destination as the mortality rate for the average journey was 10–15 per cent.

According to Herbert S. Klein, the mortality rate was 13.1 per cent for British ships, 14.1 per cent for the Dutch and 17 per cent for the few Spanish vessels that sailed.[13] However, numbers can never tell the full story. For that, we need to rely on the personal accounts of the men who sailed the ships and those who travelled on them.

Once a ship was fully loaded, it set sail from one of the West African ports for the arduous 3,500 mile journey that could take anywhere from six weeks to three months, depending on the ship and the weather. The slave-captain-turned-clergyman, John Newton, preferred to set sail at night, which was in theory more hazardous but often reduced the chance of African resistance. It is hard not to imagine the disorientation that Africans would feel as they were dragged from the dungeons that had been their homes for months on end, and herded below the decks of slave ships. Newton's plan meant that they were taken from one dark enclosure at night and forced into another dark enclosed space.

Although slavers varied in size, it became apparent that a ship's size was in direct proportion to its potential to make a profit. Consequently, during the eighteenth century, which was considered the peak period of the slave trade, slavers often carried upwards of 400 enslaved Africans, and it was not unknown for some to carry twice this number towards the end of the century. The conditions aboard these ships were appalling for all concerned, both African and sailor. However, the Africans were treated as cargo and kept below deck for most of the journey in some of the most inhumane conditions imaginable. The men were invariably chained by the leg and forced to lie side by side in cramped quarters for the majority of the passage.

Leading abolitionist, Thomas Clarkson, compared these conditions to 'books on a bookshelf' and his iconic diagram of the slaver *Brookes* clearly shows the barbarity of this environment. Ship doctors such as Alexander Falconbridge provided vivid descriptions of the sheer barbarity of the conditions on board slavers, where Africans were forced to sleep, eat, urinate, defecate and menstruate in coffin-like confines that lacked both ventilation and sanitation.

In his autobiography, Equiano describes the intolerable conditions aboard as a 'wretched situation... aggravated by the galling of the chains, now insupportable, and the filth of the necessary tubs into which the children fell and almost suffocated. The shrieks of the women and the groans of the dying rendered the whole scene of horror almost inconceivable.'[14]

The slave ship even witnessed childbirth: Ignatius Sancho, the African man of letters who joined the abolitionists, was born on a slave ship that was sailing to the Americas. Dr Falconbridge made four journeys as ship doctor before abandoning the activity to join the abolitionist Thomas Clarkson in fighting to end the slave trade. Dr James Ramsay was another who worked ceaselessly, but often in vain, to counteract the infections, infestations and diseases that thrived in such cramped conditions. Like Falconbridge, Ramsay would eventually join the abolitionists' cause.

Other ship doctors, such as a certain Arthur who served under Newton on the *Duke of Argyll*, took to drink to take his mind off the chaos below deck. Similarly, not only did bad weather curtail the enslaved Africans' opportunity to get some fresh air on deck during their limited exercise periods, but confinement in stormy conditions also increased the likelihood of seasickness. Newton took particular exception to Arthur's behaviour because his religious piety despised drunkenness (but not slave trading), and because medical men played an important role in ensuring that the human 'cargo' arrived in top condition. Each African was considered an investment that would be cashed in on arrival; the amount of cash was dependent, however, on their physical condition and the overall price at the markets.

Despite the fact that Africans were tradable commodities, their diets left much to be desired. They were often given only one meal a day – a porridge-like substance that did little to fend off scurvy or malnutrition. Similarly, they often suffered – and died – from dehydration due to a lack of drinking water.

The supposed lack of drinking water was the cause of the *Zong* incident, one of most despicable acts of the slave trade. The *Zong* was a slaver transporting Africans to Jamaica in the 1780s and its captain, believing that some of the Africans on board would not make the Caribbean alive, used the lack of drinking water as an excuse to jettison sick or dying Africans so that he could make an insurance claim.

Exercise time was one of the few opportunities Africans had to experience fresh air and daylight. It was also a chance for them to stretch their limbs while their filthy holds were cleaned. The more considerate captains washed the Africans with vinegar and limewater; many, however, left them in their soiled conditions until they arrived in the West Indies. But exercise time was considered a dangerous period for the captain and crew because it was about the only time an enslaved African was given the opportunity to revolt or escape. Captains such as John Newton ordered crew members to brandish firearms in order to dissuade mutinies.

For African women, time on deck brought the unwelcome attention of desperate, drunken crewmen, and acts of rape and molestation were not uncommon. Newton's journals attest to this and while captain he was often forced to thrash sailors who were looking to violate women. Newton was a man of many contradictions. He became a Christian in 1748 after one particularly bad experience during a slaving trip, but continued with the activity despite his newly acquired faith. His journals suggest that he performed religious services and other acts of worship above deck while the Africans were chained in their filth below. After becoming a Christian, he was consistent in his moral behaviour – if slave trading is discounted – and demanded orderly conduct from his often unruly crew.

Other captains turned a blind eye to the sexual activities on board their ships as they proved a useful diversion. If life was bad for the Africans, it was far from a bed of roses for the crewmen. The Middle Passage would be their second time at sea, having first travelled to Africa from Europe. For many crewmen, these experiences were new and unwelcome and the reality was far from the 'spin' that had been sold to them when they were encouraged to sign up.

The enslaved Africans, who had already endured the unbearable demands of a transatlantic journey, faced a life of toil in the Americas. Most were given very little time to acclimatize to their new conditions and would soon find themselves toiling in the hot sun on sugar and tobacco plantations. These plantations were an early equivalent of factories that produced one item of consumption. The Africans were unique among all the ethnic groupings that went to the Americas. Unlike travellers from Europe who arrived in the New World dreaming of how they were going to 'make it', Africans came on slavers and had work already awaiting them. The Americas were considered the land of the free for so many, but for Africans they meant only slavery.

Before embarking on this life of labour, Africans were subject to sale at auction to determine where and with whom they would work. Slave auctions would be advertised in the local press and leaflets were distributed in most public places to encourage greater interest in the sale. Public spaces were plastered with adverts listing the date of the sale, the ethnic grouping of the Africans and the ship on which they had arrived. Akin to selling livestock at a cattle auction, enslaved Africans would suffer the indignity of being prodded, pulled and inspected by potential buyers, looking for everything from scurvy to a physical disability. Most were assembled in lines with nothing to cover their nakedness but the chains which shackled them.

The early Africans who spoke Spanish or Portuguese, having come directly from Europe, probably understood what was taking place. Later on, the Africans who were brought directly from Africa had very little knowledge of European languages and would fail to heed commands to open their mouths for inspection or move certain body parts for scrutiny. Ignorant slave traders would mistakenly interpret this as insubordination and punish them.

Potential buyers were on the lookout for Africans who were in good physical shape, with an aptitude for learning quickly and the stamina to withstand the rigours of slavery, and who would cause few problems to their owners. The ablest Africans fetched the best prices at auction and slave traders went to astonishing lengths to present their 'bucks' or 'wenches' in a positive light.

It was ironic that slave traders and merchants who had been treating their 'property' with only a modicum of care during the Middle Passage suddenly decided to take an interest in the Africans' physical appearance. Africans were now subjected to rough pampering and were washed with all manner of substances to rid their skin and hair of parasites. After a serious delousing, they were smeared with oil or animal fat to highlight musculature and a healthy complexion. Equally, their toenails, fingernails and hair were all cut. Unscrupulous traders were even known to pull out any grey hairs from the heads of Africans to emphasize youthfulness or extract any teeth with abscesses to give a greater impression of vitality.

Some sales also involved selling all Africans at the same price. This was invariably described as a 'scramble' as slave owners frequently resorted to violence to acquire the fittest looking enslaved Africans. The auction was often the last place where relatives or friends would spend time together; they were sold without any consideration for family or friendship ties.

The West Indies also acted as a stopping off point for Africans in transit to North America. One of the features of the slave trade was the sheer number of enslaved Africans who arrived in North America via the West Indies. After surviving the demands of the Middle Passage, Olaudah Equiano's autobiography suggests that his first port of call was to Bridgetown, the capital of Barbados. He stayed on the West Indian island for two weeks before being taken to the then English colony of Virginia.

After being sold, an enslaved African was invariably branded again and given another name by his new owner. Africans were often given the names of powerful Greek or Roman figures such as Hercules or Julius in order to ridicule their impotence within society. Just like convicts who are given a number to replace their name, enslaved Africans were forbidden to refer to their former names. They were also prohibited from speaking their native languages or observing their religious practices. Indeed, clever planters deliberately grouped together Africans from rival or different clans to minimize any communication or potential sedition. This classic divide and rule tactic would take many forms and was usually a successful way of preventing major slave uprisings on plantations where Africans outnumbered whites by as many as 50 to 1.

When one considers that Africans were always looking to fight against their enslavement and that the whites were in a clear minority, it is surprising that there were not more African uprisings. For example, even if whites had firepower and could call upon navies stationed on various West Indian islands, in Haiti the majority population of enslaved Africans used violence to completely oust white minority rule. Perhaps the answer lies in the subtle and devious way that the Europeans played off the enslaved Africans against each other. Africans retaliated wherever possible, using cunning, guile and brute strength to attack the plantation system at every juncture.

Once on a new plantation, enslaved Africans underwent a period of 'seasoning' to help orientate them to life within this new society. This could last up to three years and involved Africans working with more experienced slaves who showed how to use the tools of their trade such as a machete, hoe or shovel. Moreover, it was hoped that the seasoned slave would quell any acts of defiance or desire to escape in the minds of newly-arrived slaves. Slave owners wished to control their slaves in order to make them servile and docile: records show, however, that neither would work as most plantations were subject to acts of passive and active resistance.

The majority of enslaved Africans ended up working on plantations in the Americas. In the British West Indies, sugar was the preferred crop and small and large plantations or estates grew it to meet the needs of sweet-toothed Europeans. Planters often sold their sugar 'through an agent in London, who purchased supplies for them and advanced money to carry them over until harvest time'.[15]

The wealth of the West Indian planter was legendary but disaster was always just around the corner. A planter was only as rich as his last harvest and the enslaved Africans that he owned. Diseases or inclement weather could destroy harvests and slaves often absconded. Likewise, the price fluctuations of sugar on the world market could mean the difference between success and failure. The sugar market was extremely competitive with

English, French and Dutch colonies all fighting to produce the most, as well as the cheapest, sugar. Agents who loaned planters money in lieu of handling their debtor's sugar often ended up owning plantations as a result of bankruptcies.

Plantations used divisions of labour similar to those used in a car plant, where one individual is charged with carrying out a particular function and little else. Most newly-arrived Africans worked as field slaves, which was considered the most onerous form of labour on the plantation. Fieldwork involved clearing land, digging and planting sugar cane – usually from dawn to dusk under the glare of the West Indian sun. To ensure that they did not slack, plantations often employed slave 'drivers' or overseers who liberally used an assortment of whips to maintain the work rate and discipline.

The busiest time on the plantation was always crop time and it was all hands on deck to turn the precious cane into sugar. Cane had to be cut before being transported to the mill where it was crushed by fearsome-looking machines to remove the juice. The juice was collected and treated with lime to remove impurities and then boiled and reduced to a dense syrupy substance. This sticky matter ran into troughs where it was allowed to cool, and subsequently placed in hogsheads – large casks – for curing. Hogsheads were perforated, allowing the molasses to drip out. The crystallised sugar was collected at the top of the hogshead and was then sent to Europe for further refinement.

Africans carried out a number of duties on sugar estates. Some worked as carpenters, masons, coppersmiths or sugar boilers, or carried out other necessary jobs on a plantation, while others laboured in the master's big house. Africans holding down skilled jobs or working in the plantation house often regarded themselves as superior to their field counterparts. The relative importance of their skills was also rewarded by certain privileges in dress and food. Slave masters were often aware of these distinctions and would threaten a domestic slave worker with demotion if they were insolent or lazy.

In most slave-based societies, a system of terror and violence was deployed to maintain order and structure. It was believed that in a society where whites were often in a minority, acts of disobedience by enslaved Africans that were not brutally punished would encourage greater defiance. Consequently, punishment became an integral part of plantation life with enslaved Africans cruelly flogged for the most minor of misdemeanours. Although they were considered to be the property of the master, owners would show little mercy in order to maintain authority on the plantation.

Such was the barbarity of behaviour towards enslaved Africans in the Americas that all European countries with colonies introduced slave laws to protect Africans, as well as to maintain law and order. However, cruel masters and overseers flouted many of these laws and it was often the case that enslaved Africans were threatened with their very lives. Runaways had half a foot, an ear or their nose chopped off while others had salt, pepper or hot oils poured onto newly-flogged skins. Africans who threatened rebellion or struck white men were killed in ingeniously wicked ways such as inserting dynamite into their orifices and lighting the fuse.

Africans had very few rights during enslavement and could never look to the courts to redress the various abuses or infringements. As the academic M.G. Smith points out, 'As is well known in the British Caribbean colonies, under the rules that prohibited the evidence of slaves against free men in a court of law the elaborate slave codes were ineffective as protection for the slave... '.[16] A case in point was that the testimony of an African was inadmissible in courts.

There are numerous accounts of overseers and slave masters brutally flogging or even killing their enslaved Africans in front of other Africans, but when such cases went to court they were dismissed because only Africans had witnessed the alleged offences. Allied to this was the understanding that slave laws in many parts of the West Indies treated Africans exclusively as their master's property and it was deemed impossible to prosecute someone for harming his or her property. In fact, the colonial authorities only punished the severest of crimes. As far as they were concerned, the planters had to use the necessary means to maintain order and productivity on their plantations.

If power corrupts, and absolute power corrupts absolutely, estate owners or managers were totally corrupted within these societies. According to one historian, 'On the estate [or plantation], the resident owner or manager was in full and complete authority with hardly any effective restraints on his behaviour. There is not a man in the world who can carry such unlimited authority over his fellow creatures without abusing it.'[17] The power to use and abuse was central to life on a plantation and although not all owners or managers were despicable, far too many were.

If Bartolomé de Las Casas, the Spanish-born Catholic friar, was largely responsible for the 'Black legend' that chronicled his countrymen's abuses, Thomas Clarkson, the British-born Anglican deacon, did a similar job in relation to abuses against Africans on plantations. As the West Indian planters were only too keen to point out, Clarkson – unlike Las Casas – had never ventured to the region to see what was happening firsthand. In some respects, he did not have to as Africans came to Britain with their masters bearing the scars of their mistreatment. Similarly, many an impressionable Englishman was forced to return home after witnessing indescribable brutality and degradation, as in the case of the abolitionist Zachary Macaulay who was sent to Jamaica as a teenager to take charge of the finances of a plantation. Macaulay was forced to leave the island after witnessing unspeakable barbarities inflicted on Africans.

The French novelist Gustave Flaubert once argued, 'There is no truth. There is only perception.' It can be argued, however, that in some instances perception can be truth, and in the case of West Indian slavery, the perception was that it was cruel and debased the rights of Africans. Abolitionists such as Clarkson found it easy to obtain information about acts of violence inflicted on enslaved Africans and argued that certain excesses were the norm on plantations.

Most estate managers or planters did not endear themselves to either Africans or their abolitionist detractors due to their arrogance, high-handedness and often disgusting behaviour. Many planters sauntered around their West Indian estates with a princely swagger. They expected Africans to address them with a deference that one associates with royalty and any act of disrespect was severely punished. Their behaviour in Britain was little better.

Many upper class Englishmen regarded certain West Indian planters to be men with money, but in truth, little breeding. However, manners were neither required nor valued in the West Indies. What counted was a white skin and money. The planters had both and were never bashful of throwing about their ill-gotten gains during their extended stays in Britain.

The writers Terence Brady and Evan Jones have argued that even some of the abolitionists were seduced by the wealth and generosity of the West Indian planters. They suggest, 'The Clapham Sect of Abolitionists… although wholeheartedly opposed, with four notable exceptions, to the "wickedness" of the slave trade, never chose to disassociate themselves from or even condemn those who grew so rich on the system they despised... These men [the Clapham Sect] bent on reform were at great pains not to insult or condemn this rich and powerful class of people...'.[18]

What applied to white West Indian men also applied to the women. From the outset of West Indian colonization, white women were scarce in numbers and, as most economists will confirm, anything in short supply will quickly increase in value. Consequently, the few white women to be found on the plantations were treated like royalty, regardless of their pedigree. It was not unknown for women of ill-repute in England to become 'ladies' of high-standing within a short time of their arrival in the West Indies. English colonial policy offered prostitutes and loose women a one-way ticket to a new life.

If the men became drunk with power, the women became intoxicated by status and quickly adopted the airs and graces normally associated with princesses. Many of these women became incapable of carrying out even the simplest of tasks for themselves and it was not unknown for an English 'maiden' to be escorted by two African women, one carrying a parasol to protect her lily-white skin from the blazing sun, and the other brandishing a fan to cool her brow.

There is little doubt that a white skin was the passport to success in these colonial societies, opening doors that were firmly closed to non-whites. These societies have been described as 'pigmentocracies', where skin colour determined your place in the social order. At the top of the colour pyramid were the rich whites who owned the plantations or held positions of authority in the country. Below them were the 'poor' whites who worked as clerks or administrators. Under them were 'mulatto' or bi-racial offspring, often the results of sexual liaisons between white men and African women. These children were sometimes acknowledged by their white fathers and given a fair degree of latitude to educate themselves or to own property. (It must be noted, however, that relationships between African men and white women were as rare as a Caribbean snow shower as Africans were routinely killed for even making advances towards white women.) Below this grouping were pure-blooded Africans, and yet even here there were distinctions, with the Creole Africans – those born in the Caribbean – looking down on those born in Africa. It was, therefore, a society of people looking down on other people, and striving to keep those people in their place.

The historian Franklin W. Knight described West Indian society as dynamic because of the constant change and movement of people and ideas. The one certainty in this society was the importance of being white, and many would recite the old adage, 'If you are white, you are alright; if you are brown, stick around; but if you are black, get back!'

In such a society, whiteness symbolized power, intelligence, beauty, freedom and wealth, while blackness represented enslavement, poverty, shame and powerlessness. Whites naturally felt superior to non-whites, and brown people felt superior to Africans because white blood coursed through their veins. The Africans who worked in the master's big house looked down on the field slaves because they worked closely with whites and dressed decently; the planter would not want them walking around his house half naked. And for the most part, they were treated decently and were not subject to working from dawn to dusk in the hot sun.

In such a colour-coded society, gradations between white and black developed, ensuring that the offspring of African and European descent was a mulatto, a quadroon was a quarter black, an octoroon one-eighth black and a quintroon one-sixteenth black (the 'quint' symbolized fifth generation removed from blackness). This fixation with colour would outlive slavery in the West Indies by centuries and only the rise of the 'black consciousness' movement in the mid-1960s would help to shake off the mentality that 'black' or African was considered inferior to 'white' and European. However, it is true that in countries with a history of slavery, people of African origin are still more likely to be found carrying out menial or manual work than in the trained professions. The same cannot be said for those of a lighter colour.

4

Blood Money

Despite the activities of Sir John Hawkins and other opportunists, England's involvement in the slave trade remained on an *ad hoc* basis until the restoration of the monarchy in 1660 under Charles II. Once on the throne, Charles wasted little time recognizing the potential of the slave trade and gave royal approval to the establishment of the Company of Royal Adventurers in 1663. This monopolistic venture gave legal sanction to the trade of human beings in Africa. Although the king and the company's wealthy backers anticipated a windfall, European wars and slapdash practices saw the venture flounder only a decade after its inception.

Studies demonstrate that the monarch could be very determined when he wanted to be and, convinced that slave trading was a money-spinner, he tried again with slave trading and established the Royal Africa Company (RAC) in 1672. The RAC had sole rights to trade in a range of commodities in Africa such as gold, ivory and spices, but the most lucrative commodity was human beings. No sooner had the RAC begun trading than West Indian planters in the British territories complained that the company's monopoly was stifling the growth of the sugar industry and its potential profits. The RAC's contract involved the transportation of 5,000 enslaved Africans per annum, a figure which failed to satisfy the huge demand for slave labour on the burgeoning plantations.

The RAC monopoly also charged the company with the upkeep of the English slave forts on the West African coast, which were vital for maintaining the country's involvement in the slave trade. Proper maintenance involved money and the RAC was loath to spend money on something that did not accrue direct profits, although they welcomed the parliamentary decision of 1730 to grant £10,000 a year for forts on the Gold Coast in order to protect the interests of its slavers.

The RAC also failed to adequately staff these forts with soldiers, administrators, priests or general labourers. Unlike the Portuguese or Dutch, only a small number of white men were ever stationed at the forts between the 1670s and 1700, and many of these whites were not English but Irish, French, Portuguese or Dutch.

One of the centrepieces was RAC's castle on the Cape Coast, less then ten miles away from the Elmina fortress. According to the writer William St Clair, a British governor at the time described the castle as 'the grand emporium of the British slave trade'.[1] The castle was captured from the Dutch in 1664 by an English armed fleet, commanded by Robert Holmes. Its impressive structure made it virtually unassailable to interlopers and its cavernous dungeons, which had the capacity to hold over 1,000 enslaved Africans, proved difficult to escape from.

It was not only the West Indian planters who envied the RAC slave-trading monopoly, as would-be entrepreneurs in England also looked on in frustration and resentment, seeing potential profits go untapped. By the late 1690s, there was more organized opposition to the RAC domination of the trade and the influential Bristol Society of Merchant Venturers lobbied parliament regularly to revoke the London company's monopoly. As a result of such powerful opposition, the company lost its lifelong right to trade in Africans in 1698, leaving Bristol and Liverpool to prise open the money-spinning English slave trade industry. But despite the RAC losing its monopoly, London continued to be the major slave port with over 80 ships leaving for the west coast of Africa as late as 1725.

The loss of the RAC's monopoly was mirrored by the efforts of entrepreneurs and adventurers throughout Europe to end such restrictive trading practices. The French Guinea Company, its Danish equivalent and other European counterparts held the respective sole rights to trade in human slaves from Africa to the Americas, and groups of merchants in these countries fought tooth and nail to break such monopolies. But what everyone wanted to get their hands on was the *asiento*, the Spanish contract or agreement to supply its colonies with Africans. The supposed riches that Spain had accrued from its colonies in the Americas had always fascinated other European countries; exaggerated tales of vessels arriving in Cadiz or other Spanish ports laden with gold, silver and precious metals not only vexed her neighbours but also gave rise to pirates and privateers in the sixteenth and seventeenth centuries.

The *asiento* was regarded as a licence to print money, and for two centuries several European countries held this right to supply Spain with its labour force. In reality, the *asiento* was fool's gold, promising more than it delivered, but this did not stop countries from fighting over it. For instance, the main aim of the War of Spanish Succession (1701–1714), which saw the English, Dutch and German collaborate, was to stop a French monarch from assuming the throne of Spain and its possessions, but it also provided England with the added incentive of obtaining the *asiento* from France. The Spanish had granted the licence to the French Guinea Company in 1702; however, under the terms of the Treaty of Utrecht in 1713, Britain secured the *asiento* for its subjects.

The *asiento* allowed the transportation of 5,000 Africans per annum for 30 years and was awarded to the South Sea Company, which was established in 1711 and had been trading with Spain's overseas territories in Latin America and the Pacific. The South Sea Company and the government talked up British financial opportunities to such an extent that its investors included the great and the good such as the author of *Gulliver's Travels*, Jonathan Swift, the legendary English poet, Alexander Pope, the writer, dramatist and friend of Swift and Pope, John Gay, Sir Isaac Newton and the founder of Guy's Hospital in London, Thomas Guy.

The South Sea Company proved to be a financial house of cards that crashed in 1720, bankrupting many of its shareholders in the infamous 'South Sea Bubble' – the name given to the financial crash that occurred over speculation in the company's shares. Sir Isaac Newton (no relation to John Newton) lost a fortune of £20,000 in the crash and reputedly mused, 'I can calculate the movement of the stars, but not the madness of men.' The company was restructured and continued its work, which included slave trading, but found that its *asiento* trade was often interrupted by British disagreements or skirmishes with Spain such as the Anglo-Spanish war that started in 1739.

The *asiento* was renewed for another four years in the Treaty of Aix-la-Chapelle in 1748 but was relinquished by Britain in 1750 on the payment of £100,000 by the Spanish government. By this time, the growth of the Transatlantic Slave Trade meant that London, Bristol, Liverpool, Lancaster, Whitehaven, Chester, Exeter and practically any western or south-coast city or town with a decent port could participate in slaving. This created a huge demand for sailors, which was met by those looking for adventure or fortune in the 'untamed' beauty of

Africa or the wild frontiers of the Americas. Others signed up for more mundane reasons such as earning a steady, honest crust in order to support their families. For others still, it was a means of escape and many a crew included bad debtors, fugitive criminals and general cut-throats.

Initially, captains had no problem assembling a crew for the year-long voyage that encompassed both Africa and the Americas. Sailors would receive an advance upon signing on, which was often used to pay off debts or support their families in their absence. Most inexperienced sailors soon realized, however, that life on the ocean waves could be monotonous and far from comfy. Slavers were built for speed, not comfort, and the conditions both above and below deck left much to be desired. The more experienced sailor knew that the least arduous leg of the journey was the relatively short passage from Europe to Africa and that the real problems would begin when they caught sight of the West African coast. The poor trade winds and fearsome tides affected sailing conditions so that important time was lost navigating a ship to the all-important slave ports.

But after struggling to make it to land, sailors then had to contend with malaria and yellow fever, to which most had little resistance. Those who did not perish from these diseases nevertheless spent months trying to shake off their debilitating effects. Parts of West Africa, such as the Bight of Benin, were known as the white man's graveyard and ditties such as '*Beware beware, the Bight of Benin: one comes out, where fifty went in!*' summed up its notoriety.

The Bight was typical of the sweltering, energy-sapping conditions that the sailors had to grapple with while their slave ship was moored at one of the many forts for months on end. Their physical condition was not helped by the fact that far too many spent this time drinking and carousing with their fellow European sailors in order to escape the boredom. Others were simply reckless and failed to heed the advice from seasoned sailors about slowly acclimatizing to local conditions. By preferring to sleep in next to nothing so that they could keep cool in the African heat, many caught chills that developed into fevers, causing numerous deaths.

The average slave trader or agent from Britain also found Africa's west coast treacherous, but they did not travel to the continent for the good of their health or for diplomatic missions. Slave traders went to Africa to make money by exchanging European goods for human beings, an abhorrent practice, albeit a particularly lucrative one. Many would never realize these dreams, but as long as this enterprise held open the hope of financial enrichment, they would continue to engage in this activity.

Human trading was a means to an end for many slave traders. They had no compunction about purchasing their fellow human beings for transportation overseas. The journals of John Newton make telling reading.

Even after his religious conversion in 1748, Newton continued his slave-trading activities and appeared untroubled about trading men and women who were made in the image of God, an idea he professed to any European who was willing to listen. Similarly, in 1758, the well-known agent Nicholas Owen recorded in his dairies his desire to make money from this honest trade. He described Africans as drunk, argumentative and licentious and appeared to use this behaviour as an excuse for his actions.

Not all slave traders or agents acting for the merchants were white. The European presence in Africa had produced a sizeable mixed-race or biracial population who were described as mulattos. These mixed-race traders were often treated with suspicion by both Africans and whites alike, as they had few allegiances to either side, and so they made perfect intermediaries for the slave trade. Henry Tucker, who was of African and Portuguese ancestry, was one such trader who accrued a small fortune acting as an intermediary on the Guinea Coast. Tucker traded with Newton during his 1750 slave-trading venture along the Guinea Coast on the slave ship the *Duke of Argyll*.

Once the slaver had its full compliment of enslaved Africans, the captain embarked on the arduous, hazardous journey to the Americas. It was on this trip that crew members came face-to-face with the full horrors of the slave trade, which dehumanized both Africans and Europeans alike. Much has rightly been said about how the trade dehumanized enslaved Africans, but less is known of the physical and psychological effects on Europeans, especially the crew of slavers. Impressionable men were often corrupted by their participation in the brutal enslavement of Africans, which often included the violation of women and murder.

Boredom was often cited as a reason for the torture of Africans, while women were raped and abused for a similar motive. And for every James Kelsall, the seaman on the *Zong* who objected to throwing Africans overboard, hundreds carried out these cruel orders like automatons.

When not abusing others, both the captain and the conditions at sea proved to be a constant menace to the crewmen. Captains flogged crewmen for even the most minor misdemeanours to maintain order on the ship. In his research to discover the true extent of brutality on slave ships, Thomas Clarkson unearthed reports of captains committing murder and torture during various legs of the triangular trade. One account involved a sailor being flogged with a heavily knotted rope. Crewmen were also forced to survive on bread and salt beef rations for most of the journey, resulting in skin diseases such as scurvy, and other diet-related problems such as ophthalmia. Additionally, some contracted diseases from Africans due to close, regular contact.

After the ship docked at one of the many New World ports, some crewmen escorted their charges from the ship to barracoons or similar enclosures where they awaited the auction. Others had the unenviable responsibility of hosing down the filthy holds before the final leg of the journey. While in the Americas, the sailors continued to drink, rum being the beverage of choice, and they frequented the numerous whorehouses that serviced sailors in the slave ports. Like Africa, conditions in the West Indies were far from perfect and places that we now regard as tourist destinations were health hazards. Akin to Africa, tropical diseases ran amok among blacks and whites alike.

Sailors also had to contend with the Machiavellian-like tendencies of captains who held the notion that some of their crew had out-served their usefulness once the ship had docked in the Americas. As most ships sailed back to Europe laden with sugar, tobacco, rum, molasses and cotton rather than human beings, fewer crew members were needed to fend off rebellions or uprisings. Captains who did not want to pay the crew the monies owed to them once they arrived in Britain did everything in their power to 'lighten the financial load'.

Some deliberately manufactured situations that made crewmen miss the boat while the more unscrupulous had sailors shot and dumped overboard somewhere in the mid-Atlantic. Records show that the mortality rate among crewmen was similar to those of the Africans; however, it is worth remembering that these numbers represent three journeys for white crewmen but only one for Africans – the journey from Africa to the Americas via the infamous Middle Passage. In the early days of the slave trade, however, many Africans were brought to Europe before being sent to the Americas as slaves.

As the eighteenth century drew on, the large pool of crewmen began to dry up and captains became less choosy about their crew. Slaving was never an occupation for a gentleman; its main requirements included a strong constitution and the ability to follow orders, and as the slave trade grew, so the crews were gathered from the lower ranks of society. The sailors making the journey through the Middle Passage would no doubt be praying for a swift, easy journey free from diseases, whimsical captains and, most of all, African-inspired rebellions.

The effect Sir John Hawkins had on the Transatlantic Slave Trade cannot be underestimated. On his first two expeditions to Africa, Hawkins deployed snatch-and-grab tactics to obtain his Africans, but on his third expedition, his approach involved methods that would subsequently be used by his successors in their dealings with Africans. Many European enslavers carefully cultivated particular African kingdoms or states with a known dislike or rivalry towards a neighbour.

On his third journey in 1567–68, Hawkins made an alliance with the king of Sierra Leone for a joint attack on the town of Bonga, which was one of the king's foes. The aim was to share the spoils of war – prisoners – between them. Over the centuries, Europeans would supply particular kingdoms with firearms to enable them to carry out slave raiding expeditions and by the early eighteenth century, the West African Bambara state of Segu (now Mali) and the kingdom of Dahomey (now the Republic of Benin) became notorious for slave raiding activities to satisfy the European lust for slave labour. In a classic case of divide and rule, these slave raiding states destabilized those that opposed the slave trade. During the eighteenth century, rulers opposing slavery were deposed and replaced by more agreeable ones.

Some European countries were keen to let African kingdoms know that those who participated in the slave trade would also receive gifts in kind, as well as the goods they had bartered for. Britain and France encouraged African rulers to send their offspring to Europe for a 'good education' as a reward for their cooperation. Unfortunately, European countries could not guarantee the protection of African boys who were sent on these educational journeys. After all, during that era it was open season for enslaving anything with a black skin and many a king's son was clapped in irons and sent off to the West Indies for a life of slavery.

During the eighteenth century, the fortunes of Africa and Britain were so linked by the Transatlantic Slave Trade that by the time Britain relinquished the *asiento* to supply the Spanish American territories with enslaved Africans in 1750, seaports such as Bristol and Liverpool had not only become the two major slaving centres in Britain, but also the leading ones in Europe. Without the major lucrative commercial rewards of London, the two cities displayed a real hunger to be part of the slave trade. Bristol, for instance, with its long history as a trading port and links to Ireland and various European cities, already had the infrastructure and knowledge to steal a march on its rivals when the slave trade was deregulated in 1698 after the repeal of the RAC's monopoly.

This development gave legal sanction to a practice that had already been taking place in Bristol for decades and enabled its ships to sail the familiar routes of the triangular trade without fear of reprimand. Figures for 1710 reveal that Bristol was nearly on a par with London for the number of ship clearances per year to West Africa and just 20 years later, it had eclipsed London to become the major slave-trading port in Britain.

Bristol's involvement in the slave trade grew in proportion to its population; in 1700 it had around 20,000 citizens but only 100 years later this figure had tripled. Its growth as a slaving port, however, brought notoriety, and proved to be a magnet for runaways, criminals, chancers, adventurers and the gullible.

The Transatlantic Slave Trade needed men and women with a range of skills to service the industry and newly arrived aspirant workers found jobs on Bristol's docks as labourers involved in the building, equipping and repairing of vessels. Others found work in industries that provisioned ships (with food and stores) or in the production of items used to barter for enslaved Africans such as copper, brass, pottery, pots and pans, clothing and any other items that could be exchanged. In addition, work could be found for the more skilled individual as a clerk, bookkeeper or administrator.

Bristol not only sent ships off to Africa but also received those making their way back from the Americas laden with the products made from the profits of slavery. By the mid-seventeenth century, Bristol was an important city for curing tobacco and refining raw cane sugar and molasses from the West Indies; by 1760, it had 20 sugar refineries and was booming in sugar-related industries such as the production of sugar and molasses pots, sugar snippers and decanters for rum as well as anything else associated with the sweet substance.

The tobacco unloaded from North America was unpacked and graded and given to those wishing to ply their trade at twisting the plant into a rope or compressing and dicing the plant for smoking. Bristol quickly became known for its tobacconists as smoking captured many a taste and wallet.

Those not succumbing to the taste of the leaf opted for its by-product, snuff, which would rival smoking in popularity later in the century. Similarly, the vast sums of money accrued from these ventures had to be stored somewhere and slaving encouraged the banking industry in the city. But although slave trading was profitable, it could also be perilous and merchants used insurers to underwrite their ships and slaves.

By the eighteenth century, Bristol had eclipsed its rivals and was responsible for half the ships leaving Britain. Its involvement in the slave trade had a considerable effect on the city, transforming it into one of Britain's foremost cities with a thriving social and intellectual life. Awash with money courtesy of the slave trade, its merchants and businessmen took every opportunity to display their wealth by building magnificent Georgian houses in leafy parts of the city. Others became philanthropists who thought nothing of donating thousands of pounds to a range of charitable causes.

Today, it seems inconsistent that someone involved in the selling of a human being overseas would then donate the profits of these sales to help his underprivileged compatriots. There is little doubt that the merchant Edward Colston is an example of this apparent contradiction. Colston was born in Bristol in 1636, but spent most of his adult life in London. His generosity knew no bounds; he donated large sums to establish almshouses and poured money into the coffers of hospitals and churches working with the city's poor. His influence is highlighted by a statue erected in Bristol in 1895 and through various sites that bear his name such as Colston Street, the Colston Hall, Colston Tower, Colstons' Girls' School and Colston Collegiate College. Colston was buried in All Saints' Church in his native city in 1721 and the memorial to the great man reads, 'this great and pious benefactor was known to have done many other excellent charities… And what he did in secret is believed to be not inferior to what he did in public.'

It was an open secret, however, that Colston was associated with the RAC, and he made huge profits from their slaving ventures in the late seventeenth and early eighteenth centuries. The monies accrued from these ventures formed the backbone of his munificence. But Colston was not alone in this apparent inconsistency; men such as John Pinney and Robert Nugent also donated large sums of the monies accrued from slave trading to charitable purposes in Bristol.

However abhorrent it may appear by today's standards, it must be remembered that slave trading was then a respectable 'trade'. After all, the king himself, Charles II, had established the RAC and a major part of its remit was to participate in the slave trade. Moreover, other members of the royal family had shares in this lucrative trading venture. With such powerful and influential backing, it was not surprising that the rich and well-connected invested in the slave trade. Indeed, many of those involved were pillars of society and of the church, holding numerous civic roles such as aldermen, mayors and deacons.

For instance, Colston was MP for Bristol in 1710, while other major merchants had contacts in parliament or were similarly parliamentarians themselves. Like all parliamentarians at the time, they used their position to feather their nests, protecting vested interests and ensuring that Bristol obtained a lion's share of the slave trade profits. They also had friends who helped to curtail the threat posed to the slave trade by the abolitionists. Even the church knew which side it could rely upon for favours and bells chimed in Bristol after an abolition bill was defeated in 1791. Moreover, many of the parishioners at St Mary's, Bristol, and other churches, were prominent slave traders. Similarly, many of the streets in the city such as Elton Road,

Codrington Place, Harford Street and Farr Lane were named after prominent slave traders.

However, Bristol lost its taste for sugar with the emergence of Liverpool as a major slaving port. Its demise as the country's leading player in the slave trade industry was due to its inability to handle the growth and development of the trade. As the demand for more enslaved Africans increased in the West Indies, slaving ships were forced to become bigger to accommodate the increased capacity. These larger boats found it increasingly difficult to navigate the Avon's contours and the shallowness of the city's port made docking virtually impossible. But Liverpool also became the dominant port because of its geography. The city was very close to Lancashire, the home of what would become the slave-produced cotton industry. Furthermore, Liverpool was far more competitive than its southern rival. Not only were the port levies cheaper but the ships were both fitted out and ready for sailing more quickly.

If figures tell a story, they present a startling case for Liverpool's rise as a slave port. In 1710, it cleared only two ships to West Africa. Some 15 years later the figure had risen to over 20, but by the 1750s, the figure was nearly 50 per annum. And by the 1780s, the combined traffic of London and Bristol was only half that of Liverpool's trade. As the eighteenth century drew to a close, Liverpool had over 60 per cent of the British trade and 40 per cent of the European trade. Its net proceeds from the African trade in 1783–93 were over £12 million, from 878 voyages and the sale of 300,000 enslaved Africans.

There is a story of a drunken actor who, while performing at the Theatre Royal in Williamson Square Liverpool, was roundly booed by the audience. The inebriated performer was heard to retort, 'I have not come here to be insulted by a set of wretches, every brick in whose infernal town is cemented with an

African's blood.' No one knows whether this account is true, but it does highlight the inextricable link between the economic growth of the city and the slave trade. Liverpool's involvement in slavery was concentrated on five main areas including slaving itself, the construction and maintenance of slave ships, manufacturing slave-produced goods such as cotton and sugar and the export of goods such as pottery, guns, brass and silk, and insurance and finance.

The city's connections with slavery and its industries can be traced to the mid-seventeenth century. Similarly, the port began to receive growing amounts of slave-produced tobacco in the 1640s and the increasing importation of raw cane sugar hastened the construction of the city's first sugar refinery by the late 1660s. That the port would soon turn its hand to slaving appeared to be a foregone conclusion: Liverpool had begun 'exporting' criminals – or those classed as 'shiftless' – across the Atlantic as soon as England had obtained its colonies in the seventeenth century. These unfortunate souls wound up working on plantations after being sold. And with one eye on the profits, the city's merchants stifled all qualms about trading in human beings, reassuring others that 'if they did not do it their rivals in Britain or even abroad would'.

Much has been written about the role the slave trade had in kick-starting the Industrial Revolution, the argument being that the profits accrued from the trade were invested in new technology and industries. Liverpool was perhaps the epitome of this, revealing the symbiotic effect that slavery had on Britain's economy and showing how slavery helped to stimulate its industries and innovations.

The development of the waterway system in the eighteenth century helped facilitate the transportation of goods from Lancashire to port cities such as Liverpool. These British manufactured items were subsequently exported to Africa or the Americas and Lancashire textiles became the apparel for an increasing number of enslaved Africans on West Indian plantations.

At the same time, Shropshire's iron was fashioned into bars which would turn out to be a staple commodity of exchange for Africans on many parts of the continent's west coast. Additionally, when not smelted into bars, British iron was made into chains, fetters, manacles, collars, handcuffs, branding irons and a whole range of devices used to shackle enslaved Africans within Africa and the Americas.

Birmingham, meanwhile, was the centre of arms manufacturing and increasing numbers were shipped to Africa during the seventeenth century. Guns developed into a further means of bartering for Africans as well as the major means of policing the trade. Europeans used guns to safeguard both their property and themselves from rivals and interlopers while Africans acquired Birmingham-made weapons to fight each other for dominance of the trade. In the latter part of the century, leading abolitionists such as William Wilberforce and John Newton would argue that a good many African wars could be attributed to the abundance of British-made guns.

Brass-made goods such as pans, pots and utensils were also swapped for human beings and British products such as sugar, rum, chocolate, snuff and tobacco became staple products for many an African chief. Moreover, the production of these items increased in direct proportion to the development of the slave trade – as did the profits. It has been estimated that the majority of the 2,100 legal Bristol passages between 1698–1807 garnered some profit for their owners, and even when Bristol had passed its sell-by date as a slave port, profits of 10 per cent could still be made.

The Tarletons were a good example of the connection between slave trading and its increasing status in Liverpool. At least three generations of the Tarletons were involved in the slave trade with Thomas being the first to engage in the practice in the 1720s. His son John, known as the Big or Great 'T', took up where his father left off and became one of the city's major players in the transportation of enslaved Africans to North America and the West Indies. He combined these financial activities with mayoral duties when he took up this civic role in 1764.

One of his four sons, Banastre, a former war hero from the American War of Independence, was also a prominent figure, becoming MP for Liverpool and using this position to vote down abolition bills within parliament. In time, Banastre Tarleton became the main opponent of William Wilberforce in his parliamentary attempts to outlaw the slave trade.

Foster Cunliffe was another slave-trading philanthropist turned civic dignitary. In the 1730s, he accrued great wealth through transporting Africans to the Americas on his slaving ships. He combined these activities with mayoral duties – he was Mayor of Liverpool on three occasions as well as President of the Liverpool Infirmary – and he also donated money to the Bluecoat School in the city. In order to maintain Liverpool's pre-eminence in slaving, he used his influence to obtain a seat in parliament for his son Ellis Cunliffe while his other son, Robert, became mayor of the city in 1758. The Earle dynasty of John Earle and his sons Ralph and Thomas, like the Tarleton and Cunliffe families, also had vast interests in slave trading in the mid-eighteenth century. In time all three would serve as mayor for Liverpool.

In the second half of the eighteenth century, Liverpool was awash with men who, like their Bristol counterparts, used their enormous slave-obtained wealth for philanthropic purposes. Men such as John Blackburne, Thomas Staniforth,

William Whalley and Arthur Heywood were known for their benevolence towards the city's poor, giving money to build or fund poorhouses, hospitals, libraries and other places of learning or correction. Involvement in the slave trade was akin to joining a private members' club or secret society, and failure to do so would jeopardize one's chances of climbing the social, civic or political ladder. For instance, between 1787–1807, all but one of Liverpool's 20 mayors were connected to slave trading in some capacity. The legacies of these slave-trading philanthropists can be found today on the city's streets which include names such Banastre Street, Cunliffe Street, Earle Street and Tarleton Street. Other eminent people are also remembered in statues or plaques dotted around the city.

The incredible profits were not the only reason for why slave trading was the preserve of the wealthy as it took someone with serious amounts of wealth to engage in this lucrative practice. Many slave-trading ventures were partnerships between several of the city's merchants who stood to make a profit or loss based on the triangular trade enterprise. Indeed, the need to meet the initial costs of such enterprises acted as one of the stimuli for the banking industry, and slave-trading merchants established many of the city's first banks.

Furthermore, merchants needed reputable establishments to deposit the vast profits obtained from slave trading. Thomas Leyland, a slave trader who served as the city's mayor on three occasions, is a good example of this, becoming a partner in one of Liverpool's oldest banks in 1802. After a series of takeovers, Leyland Bank would become the Midland Bank, which is now HSBC in Britain.

Closely linked to banking was the insurance industry, which was vital in safeguarding profits on both vessels and cargo alike.

Anything from a ship being sunk by a hurricane in the West Indies to an African-inspired slave mutiny could ruin the financial prospects of a merchant.

The slave trade was the city's main profit source and Liverpool merchants did their best to accommodate their most treasured possessions. Mayors and councillors invested heavily in a new dockside facility to keep abreast of the growth in the trade, and by the last decade of the eighteenth century, the city had numerous docks. The port also increased the number of its warehouses to store goods due for export from Britain or those arriving from the Americas. Of course, sugar, rum and cotton were central to these operations, but Liverpool docks also acted as a storehouse for goods from India that would be re-exported to the West Indies and Africa.

The slave trade stimulated a whole range of employment opportunities in Liverpool and its surrounding areas. The city became an important shipbuilding centre, which not only encouraged the timber trade, but also provided work for associated trades such as joiners, carpenters, painters and sail-makers. And as the slave trade grew more sophisticated, vessels were built specifically for the trade, helping to reduce the various legs of the journey by several weeks.

Slave traders preferred to use ships called 'Guineamen' – the name is self-explanatory – and in the second half of the eighteenth century, Liverpool became the hub of the country's slave-ship building industry. Additionally, slavers had to be provisioned for long journeys lasting several weeks, with every conceivable item provided that was needed for the journey from Europe to Africa and then further afield.

Being the country's capital and the seat of government ensured that London also occupied a prominent place in the Transatlantic Slave Trade. London merchants controlled the

RAC, making the capital the heart of the English slave trade between 1672–98. With the River Thames being such an important waterway, merchants south of the river in places such as Deptford, Greenwich and Blackheath handled the imports of sugar, rum and coffee that had arrived from the Americas. London handled over 75 per cent of the sugar trade with the 80 sugar refineries dotted around the capital turning the raw brown cane sugar into the white variety that was preferred in England.

The London-based merchant Humphrey Morice was one of many individuals who benefited from the slave trade. Becoming very wealthy through his involvement in the sugar trade, and following the customary pattern of his counterparts in Bristol and Liverpool, he took up a seat in parliament as an MP. Morice also had a banking interest – the Bank of England to be precise, for which he was governor between 1727–28. Another Bank of England governor with links to the slave trade was Sir Richard Neave, who was chair of the Society of West India Merchants. Likewise, Thomas Raikes, another director-turned- governor of the world-famous institution, had family connections to the West Indian sugar trade.

Sugar combined with slavery equalled money, and the vast profits from this activity stimulated the financial and service sector industries with banking being one of the major beneficiaries. The Barclay brothers, David and Alexander, were Quakers who shirked official denominational policy in order to make money from the slave trade, owning sugar plantations in Jamaica. The Barclay brothers married into banking families which led to the establishment of Barclays Bank, one of the world's leading financial institutions.

Another Quaker, Francis Baring, became involved in the slave business while still a youth. He would later establish a fortune that he pumped into his bank, Barings, which he founded in 1762. Baring would be knighted for his services to finance and his bank would become one of the city's leading financial institutions. Indeed, it helped to finance the Napoleonic Wars and was the personal bank of Queen Elizabeth II. However, Barings spectacularly collapsed in 1995 after rogue trader Nick Leeson ran up debts of nearly £900 million pounds at its Singapore office. The Dutch banking and insurance company ING subsequently bought the bank for the nominal fee of £1, thus bringing an end to over 230 years of the British bank's life.

The infamous Edward Colston, the slave trader-turned-philanthropist, spent more time in London than Bristol and the capital benefited greatly from his financial largesse. London was the place of choice for many merchants because it allowed them direct access to parliament and MPs who potentially supported the slave trade. It has been estimated that parliament in the late eighteenth century, which was a fraction of the size it is today, had 40 slave-trading MPs.

Someone who combined both tasks with great aplomb was William Beckford, reputedly Britain's first millionaire. Beckford acquired his vast fortune from his extensive sugar plantations in Jamaica, which made him the leading planter on the island; but he was also aware that he needed to safeguard his extensive investments. To do so, he used his wealth and influence to gain a seat as an MP in London while his brothers also became MPs for Bristol and Salisbury. The Beckfords not only ensured that all parliamentary-based anti-slavery activity was killed off early on, but they also encouraged successive governments to tighten Britain's grip on the slave trade and its related activities.

Another important figure in the capital was Robert Milligan, a wealthy sugar merchant with plantations in Jamaica and investments in the shipping side of the slave trade. Milligan used his considerable influence to encourage fellow merchants to construct the West India Docks, which would speed up the transport of goods both arriving and leaving the capital as well as circumvent fraud. The docks were opened in 1802 and Milligan's work was honoured by a statue outside a former warehouse in West India Quay which is now the Museum in Docklands.

Men like Milligan and Beckford had close links with the influential West Indian lobby who used every tactic in the book to preserve their slave-based interests. The lobby wooed MPs at social functions and in gentleman's clubs by offering them 'pieces of the financial action' in return for their support. Equally, they used newspapers, pamphlets and political speeches to indoctrinate the British public into believing that the slave trade was vital for British interests. They relied on old-fashioned self interest in order to persuade both rich and poor alike that jobs would be lost if the industry was jeopardized in any way. As the anti-slave trade abolitionists would find out to their dismay, the lobby turned into the proverbial wounded, cornered tiger when anyone threatened it and came out fighting with claws and jaws poised for attack.

The slave trade also had a tremendous cultural impact on London. German-born John Julius Angerstein amassed a vast fortune from his involvement in the insurance of slave ships travelling between Africa and the Americas. Angerstein was also an avid art collector who built up a collection that was the envy of many in Britain. After his death in 1823, his collection was purchased for the nation and would form the basis of the initial National Gallery collection.

Art and culture also benefited from the generosity of the Irish-born physician and collector Sir Hans Sloane. Sir Hans became the president of the Royal Society; he was famous for drinking chocolate – a beverage that profited from slave-produced sugar. His wife, Elizabeth, had considerable slave-based interests in Jamaica and it was this, in conjunction with his own money, that helped Sir Hans to indulge himself in his hobby of collecting coins, medals, manuscripts, books and prints. After his death, these collections became the foundation of the British Museum's collected works.

It is all too easy to make negative connections between British cities and towns and the Transatlantic Slave Trade. London certainly played a significant role in the human trade but it was also the hub of anti-slavery activity. The first anti-slavery societies emerged in London in the 1780s and most of the major agitation and political manoeuvring took place in the city. Additionally, leading African abolitionists such as Olaudah Equiano and Ignatius Sancho spent many of their years in London and their organization, the Sons of Africa, carried out their own political strategizing there. Likewise, leading Christian pressure groups such as the Clapham Sect, who were based around the wealthy village of Clapham, South London, carried out exceptional work from their base in the capital.

5

African Resistance

Despite the overwhelming odds, Africans in many parts of their continent resisted the enslavement of their people in various ways. They fought against their capture, but if captured, fought to free themselves and others. They also attacked those who were carrying out the enslavement – a tactic which has been described as 'proactive resistance', typified by the African sacking of the French slaver *Phoenix* in 1730. While the *Phoenix's* captain was bargaining for enslaved Africans on the coast of the Volta River in West Africa, others crept on board and burnt the ship. In 1768, Africans used rafts to free compatriots aboard another French slaver, the *Côte d'Or*, which was moored in the River Bonny.

British ships were not spared African attention and in 1758, the *Perfect*, a Liverpool-registered slaver, was ravaged by Africans on a rescue mission to free 300 of their countrymen. Using an assortment of weapons, Africans butchered the entire crew and made good their escape with their charges freed. Not all attempts at freedom were successful, as shown by the Calabar (Nigeria) incident in 1767 when Africans attacked seven British-registered ships. With the assistance of African collaborators, the British managed to repel all advances. When they finally gained control of the situation, they exacted swift revenge by killing all those who had taken part in the attack.

'Reactive resistance' could also be effective and those

captured by Europeans or their African flunkeys invariably came under attack. In the infamous 'Christiansborg revolt' of 1727, enslaved Africans turned on their captors and killed the governor and many of his men at a Dutch-run fort on the Gold Coast. Those not wounded in the skirmishes made good their escape while the injured fought off Dutch attempts to regain control of the fort. However, the Dutch, armed with superior weapons, eventually quelled the insurrection and exacted deadly revenge on the rebels, cutting off the heads of the captured Africans and tossing them into the sea off the African coast.

This brutal response had both a punitive and spiritual significance: it not only served as a physical deterrent, but also affected those who believed that a headless being could not be reincarnated. In time, other Europeans would hold out this sanction to those threatening to injure others or self-harm.

Some African rulers favoured diplomacy as a way of thwarting the slave trade. Nzinga Mbemba of the Congo, who was baptized into the Catholic faith and adopted the name Afonso I, sent letters to King John III of Portugal in 1526 informing him of his concerns about the slave trade and his wish to end the trade in his country. During this era, 'slavery expanded by 10,000 slaves a year. The slaves were being taken from the Kongo to Brazil...'.[1] Likewise, King Agaja of Dahomey (modern-day Benin) wrote to the British government stating his intention to end his country's involvement in the slave trade. Prior to this, Dahomey was one of the leading centres of the slave trade and would continue to be so after Agaja's reign ended.

The freedom struggle continued on board ships, with most slave rebellions occurring during embarkation or just after the ship set sail, contradicting any notion that Africans boarded slave ships as if embarking on a cruise. As such, most slave traders remained extremely vigilant during the early days of sailing.

One of the earliest recorded revolts occurred in 1532, when over 100 Africans on board the imaginatively titled slaver *Misericordia* (which means mercy in Portuguese) freed themselves during the passage from Saõ Tomé to Elmina, Ghana. Having killed most of the sailors, it is thought the Africans managed to flee to the coast. However, any belief that uprisings became more unlikely the further a ship sailed from Africa is contradicted by historical evidence, which reveals that between 1699 and 1865, over 50 major mutinies occurred on slave ships during the torturous Middle Passage. Such resistance has since been immortalized by Steven Spielberg's screen account of the events on the slaver *Amistad*.

Slaver insurgencies that did not receive the Hollywood treatment include the Marlborough Revolt in 1753, which occurred three days into the journey from Bonny, West Africa. The Bristol-registered ship was taking its 420 enslaved Africans to the Americas when the captives mutinied and took control of the ship, slaughtering most of the white crew in the process. With the assistance of a handful of their white captives, the Africans subsequently sailed the hapless vessel back to the West African coast. In another incident in 1765, the mutiny on the *Sally* occurred several hours after it had left Calabar in what is now Nigeria. The *Sally's* captain, a Mr Hopkins, threw 80 mutinous Africans overboard before eventually berthing his ship in Antigua.

The more astute slave captains remained vigilant throughout the Middle Passage and were prepared to use any means necessary in order to safeguard their property. The journals of John Newton describe an array of on-board weaponry held by his vessels to deter would-be mutineers, but captains dealt brutally with any such mutinies, taking no prisoners. A good example of this ruthlessness occurred on board the slaver *Ovartus*, whose rebel Africans had their limbs severed and heads chopped off for their part in a mutiny. Likewise, a French captain who ended an on-board rebellion hung the culprits by their feet and whipped them to death. Another captain, this time a Dutchman, lopped off the hands of an Ashanti rebel leader, and then had him hung by the arms; the unfortunate African bled to death in front of his compatriots.

But although the punishment for mutiny was severe, Africans did not desist from rebelling and it is estimated that there was at least one revolt for every nine ships leaving Nantes, France, while at least one for every ten Dutch slavers. One can also assume that ships sailing under a British flag experienced similar experiences, although evidence is hard to obtain due to British reluctance to provide accurate figures out of fear that this would deter investors.

It would be wrong to equate all seaboard resistance with uprisings, however, and many Africans undermined the system using self-destructive means. Suicide was a common feature aboard slavers and some Africans took advantage of the exercise time on deck to leap overboard and drown in the vast Atlantic. But such was the frequency of this response during voyages that crews became adept at fishing out their valuable 'human cargo' from the ocean.

Other African self-harm strategies were met with ingenious and cruel responses, such as jaw-opening contraptions to force Africans to take food. And yet little could be done to rouse those Africans who went into stasis-like conditions and died from 'melancholy'. African resistance continued in the Americas with many enslaved Africans looking to escape as they disembarked from the slave ships. The obvious problem they encountered was their new, unfamiliar environment. If they did manage to escape at this juncture, they did not have a clue where to find sanctuary.

It has been noted that most enslaved Africans in the British West Indies worked on sugar plantations, carrying out a range of activities to produce this precious commodity. Those not working on plantations carried out work around the master's house or maintained other aspects of the plantation or sugar estate. The African tendency to sing while working (something which is overstated in many television documentaries) led some white people on the plantation to believe that the Africans were happy, or at least content, with conditions in their new surroundings.

Equally, after the sugar harvest, the slave owners would give the Africans a few days 'holiday' which they used to celebrate aspects of their African heritage. Again, this joyous gaiety was interpreted as contentedness rather than an act of 'letting off steam'. But many Africans sang out of frustration at their current sufferings or sadness over the loss of loved ones and their former way of life in Africa. Other musical renditions were fused with aspects of Christianity that were picked up from clergymen and spoke of a God who would rescue them from slavery. According to the African-American theologian-historian Professor James Cone, these songs would form the basis of gospel and blues music, especially in North America.

The songs, however, also had a more subversive message, which spoke about planned escapes or uprisings from plantations, and some of the best known spiritual songs such as 'Freedom', 'Wade in the Water', 'Steal Away', 'Go Down Moses', 'Over the River' and 'My Home is over Jordan' were sung as coded messages encouraging enslaved Africans to escape. The planters often misinterpreted the singing to mean that Africans were more concerned about trusting in God and getting to heaven than escaping from the plantation or destroying their property.

Equally, clergymen assumed they were doing an effective job by instilling Africans with a form of Christianity that encouraged subservience. The reality was, however, totally the opposite and one of the best-known spiritual songs with a double meaning was the classic 'Swing Low, Sweet Chariot'. Anyone who follows rugby union will know that today it is the unofficial anthem of the English national team, but long before rugby fans sang it from the terraces, enslaved Africans sang it on plantations in the southern states of the United States in order to indicate a possible escape. Among other messages in the song, the 'Sweet Chariot' refers to a constellation of stars known as the 'Plough' that points towards the North Star, which escaping slaves used as a route to freedom in the north of the United States and Canada.

The notion that Africans enjoyed slavery was constantly propagated during West Indian enslavement. West Indian planters would frequently attack the British abolitionists for not 'understanding' the benign nature of slavery, arguing that plantation slavery was favourable to anything that would happen to them in Africa. From time to time, they would even produce an African, usually someone working in the relative comfort of the master's house, to concur with such sentiments – though it must be noted that house slaves faced Hobson's choice when it came to being content with slavery. If they disagreed, they would be condemned to harsher forms of fieldwork or face severe punishment. But the apparent compliance of some house slaves to carry out their masters' wishes has led some to believe that not all Africans resisted slavery as robustly as others. The late African- American civil rights activist, Malcolm X, compared the mindsets of the house and field slaves to highlight the complicity of some black people within an unjust, racist system. According to Malcolm X, house slaves cleaved so much to their white masters that they refused to run away when escape plots were hatched. He also suggested that when they heard about plots to burn down plantations or escape, house slaves took this information straight to their masters, who duly rewarded them while punishing the conspirators.

According to Malcolm X, these house slaves were sell-outs who would do anything for white acceptance. But although this is a compelling argument, records show that it is not strictly true. While some house slaves colluded with the slavery status quo for such reasons, others were as eager to flee plantations as their praedial or field counterparts. Indeed, many acted as snitches who eavesdropped on the dinner table conversations of whites and fed these back to their brothers and sisters on the plantations. Likewise, house slaves led many of the major African rebellions, since they had more leeway than most, and were occasionally educated by a white benefactor.

Africans arrived in the Americas generally looking to free themselves from slavery, and they deployed both active and passive resistance strategies to undermine and – in the case of Haiti – ultimately defeat slavery in the West Indies. During the early years of Spanish colonial rule, Africans joined forces with the more belligerent indigenous people to establish small communities living outside of Spanish control in places such as Jamaica and Hispaniola. It can be argued that Admiral Sir William Penn (not to be confused with his son, also called William, who founded the Quaker state of Pennsylvania in what is now the United States), had little trouble capturing Jamaica from the Spanish in 1655, but faced greater opposition subduing the Africans who had fled to the hills during the time of Spanish rule. These Africans established Maroon communities (the term Maroon derives from the Spanish word for wild), and in Jamaica, Dominica and the Dutch colonies of Suriname and Berbice in South America such communities would prove to be a thorn in the side of colonial powers for centuries to come.

Maroon settlements, which existed alongside plantations, offered a source of inspiration to brow-beaten enslaved peoples and undermined European pretensions of absolute domination. Some Maroons went on raiding parties which sacked plantations and liberated Africans in order to swell their numbers. Such was their threat in Jamaica that the British gave Maroon villages quasi-legal status, allowing them to function as virtual states within the colonial system. In return, the Jamaican Maroons agreed to desist from attacking properties and return all African runaways. The Maroons in the Dutch colony of Suriname established settlements that became liberated, autonomous communities that the Dutch authorities were never able to suppress or conquer. Established as African communities, these communities still exist today in what is now Suriname.

There is little doubt that most successful insurrections took place on larger islands with hilly, remote terrain. Such a landscape allowed Africans to establish communities that were often difficult for opponents to find, let alone penetrate. However, size was no criterion for rebellion and anywhere that used slave labour was ripe for an African revolt. In fact, plantation slavery lent itself naturally to uprisings because it was impossible to keep Africans confined indefinitely to barracoons or slaver ships because they had to work on plantations. Moreover, the insatiable craving for slave labour to expand the sugar industry led to English colonies with an 80 per cent African population by 1700.

The relatively small island of Barbados was one of the first English territories to experience an African revolt. In 1649, enslaved Africans hatched a plan to slaughter the island's entire white population and establish what would have been an African-run colony. The Africans' ambitions were only thwarted after the authorities discovered their plans and subsequently executed the ringleaders.

However, it was during the eighteenth century – the zenith of the Transatlantic Slave Trade – that sustained insurrections on plantations were most obviously witnessed. In Jamaica alone, the island witnessed two Maroon wars and six major uprisings. In 1730, Maroons – led by the resourceful Cudjoe and his brothers – fought a nine-year war with the British, resulting in a peace treaty granting Jamaican Maroons both their freedom for life and 1,500 acres of land on the island.

In 1736, Africans in Antigua dismissed any notion of a peace treaty with the British and instead hatched a plot to wipe out the island's white population. The conspiracy involved destroying the governor's residence and razing neighbouring plantations. However, the plan failed and just less than 100 conspirators were executed. Then, in 1760, Jamaica was once again the setting for a revolt with the Tacky Rebellion. Tacky, an enslaved African, led a mass uprising in the eastern part of the island but the British eventually snuffed out the rebellion, executing around 400 insurgents in the process. That same year, the tiny island of Nevis also experienced a sizeable African uprising that saw lives lost and property damaged.

In 1763, on what is now the territory of Guyana, Cuffy – an educated house slave – led the Berbice Slave Revolt. Cuffy had called on the governor to release all enslaved Africans but after several rebuffs took matters into his own hands and encouraged his compatriots to take control of the Dutch territory. The

Africans quickly destroyed plantations and killed Dutch settlers in the process but the Dutch responded with warships and troops – including regiments from other European countries – in order to put down the uprisings. In a final act of defiance, Cuffy took his own life rather than risk being captured. The tiny island of Montserrat, known for its volcanic activity, also experienced a seismic human upheaval, this time in 1766, when Africans went from plantation to plantation on 'search and destroy' missions.

However, the mother of all rebellions took place on the French part of the island of Hispaniola, known as St Domingue (what is modern-day Haiti), in 1791. It can be argued that this rebellion was the single most important event to happen within the history of the West Indies and it needs to be addressed to show how Europe reacted to the greatest African threat to its control. The most fascinating aspect of the St Domingue revolt was the way in which it mushroomed from an insurrection into an outright revolution, which resulted in St Domingue becoming only the second country in the Americas to obtain its independence.

The St Domingue independence struggle has its roots in the French Revolution of 1789. In the two years since that event, the ideas of liberty, brotherhood and equality had made their way across the Atlantic to St Domingue, France's jewel in its West Indian Crown. The wealth of the island was based on sugar, and the lifestyles of many of the rich whites (*grande blancs*) matched those of the French aristocracy. In fact, the wealthy St Domingue whites were notorious for their penchant for the latest luxury goods from Paris and their trips to the French capital involved an almost unending round of shopping and socializing. But like all successful sugar economies at the time, St Domingue's wealth was dependent on slave labour and by 1791 the colony had well over half a million Africans who outnumbered their white counterparts in some sections of the country by at least 50 to 1.

The St Domingue rebellion began in 1791 as a large African insurrection, which over the course of the next few years became a struggle to rid the territory first of slavery and then of French colonial rule. Central to the initial uprising was François-Domingue Toussaint L'Ouverture (L'Ouverture meaning 'the opening'). The Trinidadian historian C.L.R. James has written a very detailed description of Toussaint. According to James, he 'was very small, ugly and ill-shaped, but though his general expression was one of benevolence, he had eyes like steel and no one ever laughed in his presence. His comparative learning, his success in life, his character and personality gave him an immense prestige among all the Negroes who knew him, and he was a man of some consequence among enslaved Africans long before the revolution. Knowing his superiority he never had the slightest doubt that his destiny was to be the leader, nor would those with whom he came into contact take long to recognise it'.[2]

Toussaint's vision involved freedom for all Africans and an end to slavery in the territory. Such was his military and tactical know-how that he simultaneously waged war while holding negotiations with the French. In a moment of cunning genius, he forged allegiances with the authorities in the Spanish-controlled part of the island, knowing that European rival powers would use the disarray as a pretext to invade the sugar rich territory. His plans were borne out when in late 1793 the British invaded the coastal sections of the island in an attempt to seize control of the country. With the assistance of his generals, Jean Jacques Dessalines and Henri Christophe, Toussaint beat the British back from several Haitian towns. After suffering heavy losses, aided by several lethal doses of yellow fever, the British were forced to withdraw from the island in 1798.

Another facet of Toussaint was his ability to negotiate with potential foes in order to fight the common enemy. He co-opted influential leaders from St Domingue's mixed-race or 'mulatto' grouping and persuaded generals such as André Rigaud to fight against French colonial rule and British interventions. However, he was aware of Rigaud's disloyalty and was prepared for his attempt to seize power, which occurred in 1799 with the assistance of Alexandre Pétion and Jean Pierre Boyer. Toussaint managed to quell this mulatto-led revolt by the turn of the century and in 1801 he tightened his grip on St Domingue, turning it into an autonomous state. However, his old enemy Napoleon, who once again had designs on the former territory, thwarted his plans for immediate independence.

In 1802, Napoleon dispatched his brother-in-law General Charles Leclerc to quell the African-led revolution and restore order. The French had greater military success than the British and they succeeded in forcing Toussaint into making a number of misjudgments. Leclerc invited Toussaint to talks but used the opportunity to seize the St Domingue leader and send him to France in chains, where he would eventually die in a cold dungeon in 1803.

However, his capture would renew hostilities between Leclerc and the Haitians, and once again yellow fever came to the Africans' aid, killing Leclerc and many of his cohorts. It left the remainder of the French forces so weakened that they were no match for the army commanded by Dessalines and Christophe, and in 1804 the country was declared independent and given the name Haiti, with Dessalines chosen as governor for life.

Haiti was the first black sovereign nation in the Americas. It was also the first West Indian territory to declare its independence and only the second country to gain self-rule in the western hemisphere. The Haitian Revolution had a tremendous impact on black and white psyches alike. Throughout the Americas, Africans had clear evidence that uprisings could lead to real freedom and black rule, dispelling notions that the best they could hope for were communities of resistance hiding out in the hills. The Haiti experience taught Africans that concerted, determined efforts could result in their freedom.

News of the revolution spread like wildfire; it was fanned by the tongues of whites, among whom it was the number one topic of conversation. Table talk concerned how to prevent another St Domingue incident and eavesdropping Africans were ever eager to relay this information to their compatriots. Furthermore, Simón Bolívar, the Venezuelan-born leader who was largely responsible for freeing great sections of South America from Spanish rule, was deeply inspired by the Haitian Revolution. The Haitian leader, Pétion, offered Bolívar sanctuary in 1815 as well as the assistance of troops and other forms of help if he freed the enslaved Africans within Venezuela.

Like St Domingue, most West Indian territories controlled by the British had an overwhelming African slave population and a tiny white minority. These societies functioned well only if Africans cooperated but Haiti was a good example of what could happen if they did not. However, Africans did not always have to use such obvious violence to destabilize these societies and some would use more subtle means to undermine the running of plantations. This included *petit marronage* – individuals running away from a plantation either temporarily or permanently.

Any human absence from a plantation hit the owner hard and Africans sometimes fled estates to avoid a whipping or to demand better working conditions. Planters were rarely known for their leniency and mercilessly flogged Africans for the smallest of misdemeanours, so Africans who had blundered would take a leave of absence until the wrath of their owner subsided. Others fled plantations, pledging only to return on guarantee of better working conditions or food rations. This sophisticated response was risky and more often than not resulted in punishments rather than improvements; during the eighteenth century, laws relating to the punishment of enslaved Africans ensured that they faced limb amputations if they were absent from a plantation for more than 30 days.

Other forms of passive resistance included 'go slows', undue carelessness and feigning dim-wittedness in order to challenge the running of plantations. Another strategy involved deliberately damaging property or pretending to be ill to avoid arduous tasks. Additionally, Africans continued with their bias for self-harm in the Americas as pregnant women aborted their unborn or newly-delivered babies to avoid bringing a child into a world of slavery.

African-led resistance was then a fundamental part of the history of the Transatlantic Slave Trade, and it took many forms. Resistance usually involved violence to some extent and Africans regarded force as very much part of the solution to their freedom. According to Michael Crayton, Africans 'seized the weapons that were to hand and used the aid of whatever allies they could find'.[3] In today's world we often equate violence with the natural response of terrorists, yet historically it has often been described as the 'language of the unheard'. Africans often resorted to violence because there was no other way for their voices to be heard. Similarly, western society today condemns violence as a means of liberation and yet it is willing to tolerate 'wars' in order to bring tyranny to an end. Historical records also show that the major Maroon uprisings in Jamaica were described as 'wars', while the Haitian Revolution is often described as the 'St Domingue War of Independence'.

The most infamous rebellion of them all in the West was the American War of Independence in the late eighteenth century, which was a bloody series of encounters fought to liberate the Americans from British 'tyranny'. And within the past 100 years, most Western countries have engaged their secret service operatives in covert activities to destabilize brutal regimes or dictatorships, particularly during the prolonged 'Cold War' era. It could be argued that such examples enable us to equate these activities with the subversive tactics used by the Africans to undermine slave-based regimes.

In the final analysis, Africans had the most to lose during chattel enslavement and the most to gain by obtaining their freedom. While Europe procrastinated about the legitimacy of chattel slavery and whether Africans had the capacity to live as free men and women, Africans took the situation into their own hands and fought passionately for their liberty.

6

A Change is Going to Come

There is a tendency to associate the abolition of the Transatlantic Slave Trade almost exclusively with polite debates in parliament or rousing speeches from pulpits in churches or assembly rooms. Such is the penchant for this traditional interpretation of anti-slavery activity that the efforts of enslaved Africans are seldom factored into the equation of the abolition movement.

In recent years many historians have begun to tell the story of Africans who worked alongside their white compatriots in order to raise awareness of the slave trade in the second half of the eighteenth century, and yet the African freedom movement began at the outset of chattel slavery many centuries earlier.

Unlike their Quaker or evangelical counterparts, enslaved Africans had no access to the ballot box or the debating chamber to discuss the niceties of slavery. Their main means to end slavery invariably involved violence. History tends to applaud movements or transformative measures that use the ballot rather than the bullet, and far too many commentators seem to dismiss slavery-related revolts as random acts of violence perpetrated by desperate people rather than calculated, sustained plans to bring an end to enslavement.

Allied to this misinterpretation of history is the misconception that Africans waited for European abolitionists to free them from slavery. Yet if we are ready to accept the link between African uprisings and the eventual abolition of slavery, it is hard not to accept that these responses must be placed alongside the work of European abolitionists as both parties clearly contributed to the destabilization and cessation of chattel slavery. Moreover, as in the European abolition movement, the African version had its heroes who fought against the slave trade and chattel enslavement in Africa and the Americas – men and women such as Nzinga Mbemba of the Congo, King Agaja of Dahomey (modern-day Benin), Nanny and Cudjoe in Jamaica, Cuffy and Quamina Gladstone in Guyana and Bussa in Barbados.

Unlike their European counterparts, however, these figures tend to be celebrated only in their own countries, as the traditional Western interpretation of abolition seems to leave out their story. This is an oversight because many of these men and women lost their lives in the struggle to bring about African freedom – this could never be said of their equally brave European equivalents. The deaths of these freedom fighters typify the sacrifices that Africans were prepared to make to end slavery, and explode the myth that Africans waited on Europe for freedom.

Unlike the Africans, who had a vested interest in fighting the Transatlantic Slave Trade from the outset, many in Europe were particularly slow to turn their attention to the plight of Africans. The enslavement of Africans was not a primary concern for many of Europe's philosophers and thinkers who were busy discussing religious reformation, enlightenment, the earth's place within the solar system or any other ideas or beliefs gripping Europe. This is not to say that they were totally disinterested in Africans but rather that they were disengaged.

Initially, the Transatlantic Slave Trade was out of sight and so 'out of mind'. When it did become a topic of conversation or a point for debate, scholars and religious thinkers were far from enlightened in their ideas and often fell back on crude stereotypes and general ignorance in order to dismiss the subject. Others would condemn the idea of slavery but nevertheless invest heavily in the slave trade.

It would be no exaggeration to suggest that the European attack on the Transatlantic Slave Trade was comparable to the breaching of a vast damn using a pickaxe; at first nothing appears to be happening, then a few slabs of the structure are displaced before eventually the whole structure gives way. The question that still vexes many historians is 'who wielded the pickaxe first'? Some argue that the Religious Society of Friends, better known as Quakers or Friends, must take the credit for this.

The Quakers have often been described as the unsung heroes of the abolition movement as their contribution to the struggle has either been ignored or undervalued. They wrote the first pieces of anti-slavery discourse, yet others who lifted vast sections of their work, such as Thomas Clarkson, received the credit. They established the first abolition committee, but only the names of the Anglican members are remembered. In fact, a Quaker called Thomas Fowell Buxton was largely responsible for ending slavery in the British colonies, yet the evangelical Anglican William Wilberforce still gets much of the credit.

Quakers have always focused on 'behind the scenes' work, providing the ideas, inspiration and finance for a campaign and leaving others to take the plaudits. Quakers have always empathized with the dispossessed and marginalized because they themselves experienced fierce persecution for their beliefs during the early years of their existence in the 1650s. Quakers refused to take oaths of allegiance and were often imprisoned for their refusal to do so. George Fox, who is generally considered the founder of the Quaker movement, was jailed on

A slave ship fitted out prior to embarking on the Triangular Trade

Enslaved Africans forced below the deck of a slave ship

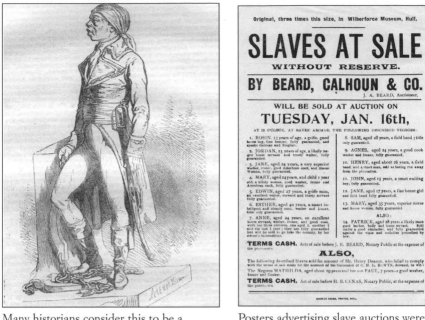

Many historians consider this to be a representation of Toussaint L'Ouverture

Posters advertising slave auctions were commonplace in the Americas

Not all slave auctions were so 'civilized'. Africans were invariably paraded in a near-naked fashion while would-be buyers examined them like cattle

ii

Shackled enslaved Africans enduring the long march from the African interior to the coast

The cultivation of sugarcane under the tropical sun was arduous, soul-destroying work

iii

Above: Transatlantic slavery was built on terror and violence. Enslaved Africans were flogged for even the most minor of misdemeanours

Right: Slavery was synonymous with violence. In Haiti, Africans used violence to end a violent system

William Wilberforce, the Hull-born MP, who led the parliamentary fight to end the slave trade

Olaudah Equiano, the one-time enslaved African who bought his freedom and became a best-selling writer and famous anti-slavery campaigner

Above: The Wedgwood anti-slavery Cameo, designed by Josiah Wedgwood, became the iconic emblem of the anti-slavery movement

Left: The apprenticeship system, which replaced slavery, was slavery by another name – hence the need for a campaign to end the system

many occasions for his refusal to swear oaths of various kinds. While on trial for blasphemy in 1650, Judge Bennet ridiculed Fox's demand that he should 'tremble at the word of the Lord' by denouncing Fox and his faction as 'Quakers'.

The Quakers were an extremely egalitarian organization that recognized and affirmed the roles of women in the seventeenth century and upheld the concept of 'hat honour'. Simply put, hat honour was a refusal to bow and take off their hats to anyone, regardless of status, title or rank. Nor would they address anyone as 'sir', 'madam' or 'your majesty'. It is said that when William Penn, one of the prime movers of the movement, met with King Charles II he refused to doff his hat or observe the usual niceties associated with a royal encounter. The king must have been in a good mood that day because there was no account of Penn being punished for his insolence. Others, however, were not so lucky and were jailed for not swearing an oath of allegiance to the king, for refusing to support his army and for criticizing any action associated with violence or cruelty.

The Quakers were rightly considered to be a radical group in the seventeenth century; while most believed in the divine right of kings, Friends advocated that everyone was 'equal in the sight of God, and capable of receiving the "light" of God's spirit and wisdom', which obviously included enslaved Africans. Many Quakers such as Fox and Benjamin Lay denounced slavery as morally wrong, and the violence associated with it contravened their beliefs on cruelty. Not all Quakers, however, adhered to these views and some owned slaves and had financial interests in the Transatlantic Slave Trade.

Like most Christian groups who would follow them, the Quakers realized that the Bible provided much food for thought on the topic of slavery and the slave trade. The Quakers were not the first, and by no means the last, to realize that the Bible appeared to condone as well as condemn slavery. This created great confusion among those who usually looked to the good book for an authoritative position on moral or contentious issues, as it appeared to mirror world history in so far as it contained clear references to slavery. Scriptural verses in the Old Testament, especially the books of Exodus, Leviticus and Deuteronomy, seemed to condemn the enslavement of the Hebrew people but suggest that it was acceptable for Hebrews to enslave others. The apostle Paul's epistles in the New Testament equally appeared to condone slavery, particularly the book of Philemon.

Both before and after the Reformation, the Catholic Church grappled with the issue of slavery and freedom for all with various popes both condemning or condoning the human trade via edicts issued from the Vatican. Pope Nicholas V (pope from 1447 to 1455) issued a papal bull to 'attack, subject and reduce to perpetual slavery the Saracens, Pagans, and other enemies...[on] the coast of Guinea (Africa)'. Nearly 40 years later, Pope Innocent VIII received 100 Moorish slaves from King Ferdinand II of Aragon. The pope decided to share his good fortune with colleagues and made presents of the slaves to his cardinals and other officials.

Others denounced the slave trade as wicked and issued edicts denouncing the practices. In 1537, Pope Paul III issued the bull, *Sublimis Deus*, which condemned the slavery of Indians but also of 'all other peoples'. Similarly, almost a century later, Pope Urban VIII issued a bull that 'prohibited slavery of any kind among the Indians of Paraguay, Brazil, and the entire West Indies'. These edicts, however, failed to have any impact on the coast of West Africa or the burgeoning colonies in the West Indies, especially in relation to Africans. At a time when papal authority was unquestioned in many parts of the then known world, it would be interesting to ascertain whether the threat of excommunication for slave trading or slave holding would have concentrated Spanish or Portuguese minds. Unfortunately, various popes were aware that slavery-related monies found their way into Vatican coffers, and were comforted by the fact that all the Africans sailing from Catholic-controlled African seaports had been inducted into the faith.

Catholic popes, as well as other important thinkers of the time, knew that slavery was as old as time and took many forms. Although slavery is associated with the removal of liberty and the denial of human rights, humanity has always struggled with the concepts of equality and freedom. The Greek philosopher Aristotle argued that 'humanity is divided into two: the masters and the slaves', and the apostle Paul argued that slaves must serve their masters with fear and trembling.

Slavery was entrenched throughout Europe right up until the Middle Ages. The Domesday book of 1086 suggests that one in eleven English people were slaves, while in the thirteenth century, Alfonso X of Spain compiled *Las Siete Partidas* or Seven Divisions, which included laws governing how slaves were treated in Spain. Its neighbour, Portugal, the father of slave traders, finally abolished slavery on its shores in February 1761.

It seems that most societies have experienced slavery in some form or another, and philosophical, religious and legal arguments could be advanced to both justify and condemn this activity. However, there was something singularly depraved and particularly sinister about the Transatlantic Slave Trade that sets it apart from anything the world had seen up to that point. Prior to the Transatlantic Slave Trade, there was no historical precedent for millions of chained men, women and children being held in the cramped holds of ships for weeks on end during transportation across the Atlantic to work on plantations or excavate mines. The closest comparison to slave trading in the Bible is the Genesis account of Joseph being sold into slavery by his brothers. Joseph was sold to merchants because his brothers deemed this to be a better alternative to murder, but jealousy rather than money or labour exploitation was the major motivation for their actions.

Chattel enslavement so dehumanized Africans, turning them from human beings into human cargo, that it is possible to compare the human trade with that of the silk or spices trades from the east or the cotton or sugar trades from the Americas. As a result, it was entirely consistent for some to condemn the system of slavery and yet support the African slave trade because Africans were mere commodities to be bought and sold. The noted English thinker John Locke perfectly epitomizes this. He published works condemning slavery and is seen as part of the proto-abolition movement, yet he was one of the major investors within the RAC.

The Quakers were one of the first groups to argue that Africans were made in the image of God, and were part of God's creation and inheritors of the spiritual and material freedoms won for them by Jesus Christ's sacrificial death. They questioned how, if an African could become a Christian, a fellow Christian who is made in the 'same' image could exploit or brutalize that individual.

Other anti-slavery proponents opted for the economic approach which set aside issues of morality and appealed to hard-headed sensibilities, namely money and profit. The central thrust of these arguments was that slave-based labour was unprofitable when compared to free labour. The Scottish thinker, John Millar, was one of the first to put forward such arguments in *The Origin of the Distinction of Ranks*. The country's attention was drawn to such ideas by Adam Smith's seminal book *Wealth of Nations*, in which he said, 'From the experience of all ages and nations, I believe, that the work done by free men comes cheaper in the end than the work performed by slaves. Whatever work he does, beyond what is sufficient to purchase his own maintenance, can be squeezed out of him by violence only, and not by any interest of his own.'[1]

But Smith was not alone in thinking that slave labour was wasteful and inefficient. It was expensive because Africans had to be purchased in the first place, and although they were paid little in wages, they had to be fed, housed and clothed. Likewise, their families became the responsibility of the plantation or estate owner rather than the head of the household. Equally, slave labour was coerced labour and very few enslaved Africans (or anyone else for that matter) were prepared to give a 100 per cent's worth of effort. Slave labour within the confines of a plantation had very few personal incentives for enslaved Africans – there was little motivation to work hard to support one's family or to purchase a house or a plot of land.

While some in Europe had become enlightened about the humanity of Africans and their commonality with Europeans, others were encouraging ideas of African inferiority, both intellectually and morally. During the late eighteenth century, European intellectuals such as Johann Friedrich Blumenbach carried out 'scientific' investigations examining the differences between human groups. Blumenbach's study of human skulls led him to separate the human species into five 'races': the Caucasian/Georgian or white race, the Mongolian or yellow race, the Malayan or brown race, the Negro or black race and the American or red race.

According to Blumenbach, 'The skin of the Georgians is white and this colour seems to have belonged originally to the human race… but it can easily degenerate into a blackish hue.'[2] In his opinion, the African was the lowest of all the races.

Blumenbach's theories echoed those of Edward Long, whose infamous *History of Jamaica* helped to shape the opinions not only of the West Indian island, but also of Africans themselves. Long was born in Britain in 1734 and arrived in Jamaica in 1757. In his book, published in 1774, Long argued that 'When we reflect on the nature of these men and their dissimilarity to the rest of mankind, must we conclude that they are of a different species of the same genus?'³ Long would conclude that Africans were not only ugly, but had more in common with apes than white men. To these physical attributes, Long added character stereotypes by suggesting that the African was crafty, uncouth, wicked, superstitious, dangerous, lazy, insolent and violent. These influential ideas would help to shape the way Africans were treated during the time of slavery and practically every negative attribute listed by Long would characterize western attitudes of Africans right up until the twentieth century.

Nevertheless, long before racial science had taken a grip on European minds, many English explorers held the belief that the existence of indigenous slavery – and the lack of Christianity – in Africa was a result of some moral or spiritual failing on the part of its people. The more religious explorers would look at the supposed Curse of Ham found in Genesis 9:25 for an explanation of why Africa was the way it was.*

The Genesis interpretation and a general lack of interest in the spiritual well-being of Africans accounts for the tardiness of strategic and sustained British missionary activity on the continent until the nineteenth century. The Great Commission of Jesus (Matthew 28:18–20) commands all his followers

---

* The Curse of Ham recounts the Old Testament figure Noah appearing to 'curse' one of his sons, Ham, for not averting his glance when his father lay naked. The curse rendered Ham a slave to his two brothers. Thousands of years later, Europeans made the link between Ham and Africans and suggested that their enslavement was biblically endorsed.

to make Christians of unbelievers. Although it was possible to question their motives, the Portuguese took the religious welfare of their enslaved Africans very seriously. They built chapels and cathedrals everywhere they went in Africa, and the priest was very much a part of any expedition or colonial activity on the continent.

Conversely, the English displayed characteristic reserve during those early years and kept their interactions Bible-free. Initially, the Portuguese demanded that every enslaved African leaving the continent in one of their ships had to be baptized into the Christian faith but the English were never so precious about the religious affiliations of the Africans they shipped across the Atlantic. Missionary-based activities as we know them only took place during the scramble for Africa, when Khaki-clad Victorians with pith helmets carried Bibles and British culture across to Africa.

By the mid-eighteenth century, many in Britain were familiar with Africans and their plight courtesy of wealthy West Indian planters bringing their enslaved Africans with them on British sojourns. It has been estimated that up to 15,000 Africans lived in the country, many of whom were enslaved Africans, runaways or free people. Absentee planters or landlords took every opportunity to flaunt their wealth in the metropolis and an enslaved African was one sign of this opulence; the saying 'as rich as a West Indian planter' became a term to describe the wealth of absentee planters.

Absentee planters such as William Beckford, arguably Britain's first millionaire, left their properties in the West Indies in the hands of solicitors, accountants and estate managers, to live royally in Britain. Such was the popularity of bringing Africans to Britain that the black population numbered several thousand in the mid-eighteenth century.

Former enslaved Africans who came to Britain with their masters are remembered today in a variety of ways. Bristol has Peros Bridge in honour of Pero (Jones). Pero was born in the West Indies but taken to Britain in 1783 by his master John Pinney, a West Indian plantation owner and sugar merchant. The unfortunately named Samboo arrived in Britain in the 1730s and lived in the small slave port city of Lancaster. After his death he was buried in a field which was imaginatively named 'Samboo's field'.

However, the status of these Africans had yet to be determined. There is little doubt that many of them felt aggrieved when they realized that the white servants belonging to their master were both free and received wages. The Africans, however, had exchanged a hot plantation house for a colder British one, and experienced little of the benefits enjoyed by the whites in their masters' service. Consequently, many absconded and took their chances on the cold, dirty streets of London. Unsure of whether they still had legal rights to their runaway slaves in Britain, West Indian planters called on the government to provide legal guidance.

Part of the planters' concern revolved around the notion that Africans automatically became 'free' if they converted to Christianity in Britain. Although the resulting Yorke-Talbot Ruling clarified that enslaved Africans would remain the property of their masters even if they became Christians in Britain, Africans continued to believe that conversion equalled freedom.

As the law took its time to decide the status of Africans, religious groups such as the Quakers began to take a closer look at the slave trade and the horrors of African slavery. As we have already seen, the Quaker contribution to the abolition movement has often been downplayed or ignored. Akin to African participation, the Quakers are often regarded as peripheral figures when in reality they remain at the heart of the story. Part of this lack of profile is that their measured, strategic approach had less cache than that of an eloquent, dapper William Wilberforce at the dispatch box or the flair of a dandy-looking Granville Sharp in a courtroom.

However, as early as 1671, George Fox encouraged his fellow congregants to desist from owning slaves and by 1696 Quakers in Pennsylvania had officially declared their opposition to the introduction of enslaved Africans. In the following century, Quaker opposition to slavery increased with disquiet, giving way to disgust over the human trade and any Friend's involvement.

The two main centres of 'Quakerdom' – Philadelphia and London – debated the subject at their annual meetings in the 1750s, helped by the intervention of one of their brethren, the former school teacher Anthony Benezet. Benezet's influential book *Some Historical Account of Guinea* (1772) became required reading for abolitionists on both sides of the Atlantic and the great British abolitionist, Thomas Clarkson, liberally helped himself to many of the Quaker's ideas. When not railing against slavery in his writing, Benezet used persuasive arguments to convince fellow believers that one could not be both a good Quaker and slave trader or owner.

Benezet's influence led to a large-scale Quaker divestment in all slave-related activities. Quaker financiers withdrew from all slave-trading activities and brethren freed their slaves on the Caribbean island of Tortola half a century before emancipation. Likewise, Quakers were responsible for the establishment of nearly every early anti-slavery society on both sides of the Atlantic.

With such a sterling commitment to abolition, it may come as a surprise to learn that not all Quakers were anti-slavery. The Quaker record was partially compromised by renowned figures such as the Barclay Brothers, David and Alexander, whose links with slave trading resulted in the establishment of Barclays Bank. Additionally, the Quaker merchant Robert King was the last slave master of the former enslaved African turned abolitionist Olaudah Equiano. Similarly, the slaver *Willing Quaker* plied its trade between Boston and Sierra Leone in 1793. However, the most damning indictment against the Quakers was their refusal to accept Africans as members of their organization. It would appear that Africans were too good for slavery but not good enough for Quaker meetings.

Other religious groupings joined the Quaker's denunciations of slavery as inhuman and incompatible with a Christian doctrine, recognizing that all humans are made in the image of God. Chief among these groups were the evangelicals, whose growth in Britain was undoubtedly due to the influence of George Whitefield and John Wesley, whose writings and preaching revitalized the church in the second half of the eighteenth century. Both held strong views on slavery and slave trading. In 1774, Wesley went on to write his influential pamphlet *Thoughts Upon Slavery*, in which he used scripture and persuasive arguments to denounce the 'vile practice' of slavery. In Wesley's opinion, 'If, therefore, you have any regard to justice, (to say nothing of mercy, nor the revealed law of God), render unto all their due. Give liberty to whom liberty is due, that is, to every child of man, to every partaker of human nature. Let none serve you but by his own act and deed, by his own voluntary choice. Away with all whips, all chains, all compulsion! Be gentle toward all men; and see that you invariably do unto every one as you would he should do unto you.'[4]

This pamphlet had a massive impact and it is said that, having read *Thoughts Upon Slavery* at his Olney vicarage, John Newton's eyes were opened to his former activities in slave trading and from that moment, he was determined to make amends if the opportunity presented itself. However, Wesley's old sparring partner, Whitefield, would later change his tune after securing a preaching post in Georgia, USA, a slave-based state then under British rule. He owned approximately 50 enslaved Africans and crossed swords with Wesley about the importance of slavery to Georgia's economy.

Although evangelicals became known generally for their personal piety, zeal for the Bible and commitment to conversion, they also shared the Quakers' concern for social justice and the freedom of Africans was high on their agenda. The emergence of evangelical Christianity changed the socio-political and religious landscape of Britain in the second half of the eighteenth century. There was hardly a town or city that did not fall under the influence of 'Methodism' as some called it during that era, and men such as Wesley have been credited with 'saving the nation's morals and delivering it from the clutches of revolution'. The historian Asa Briggs describes how 'by 1780 the new "vital religion" [of the evangelicals] had burst its way, appealing to men and women who were dissatisfied with "rational Christianity" of both church and chapel or to those who had previously known little of the claims of religion, rational or otherwise'.[5]

In Briggs' opinion, Wesley played a crucial role in changing lives and his influence was particularly strong among the poorer classes living in the new industrial towns. More importantly, it helped to turn many of the 'adherents' of Methodism into 'critics of the social and political order',[6] latching onto Wesley's writings and preaching against slavery and joining the anti-slavery movements. It was no coincidence, therefore, that the strongholds of 'Methodism' were also the centres of the anti-slavery movement.

The Quakers and 'Methodists' were part of the non-conformist movement in Britain that saw the slave trade as both a moral and a religious issue, connected to 'sin' and an individual's commitment to upholding the truth. Other denominations such as the Moravians also began to question the right of one human being owning another.

The issue of ownership in Britain would come to the fore in 1765 with the legal case of the one-time enslaved African, Jonathan Strong. Strong had been taken to Britain in the 1760s by his master David Lisle, a white Barbadian lawyer. For reasons that are still unknown, Lisle brutally pistol-whipped the teenager and left him for dead on one of London's streets. Strong would have perished were it not for the intervention of one Granville Sharp, who passed Strong's badly beaten body on his way to his brother's surgery. His brother, William Sharp, was the king's personal physician, and gave Strong life-saving treatment before sending him to St Bartholomew's Hospital to convalesce.

Once back on his feet, the Sharp brothers provided Strong with financial assistance before finding him work in London. Life appeared to be going well for young Strong until he had the misfortune to run into his former master on a London street nearly two years later. Lisle, who was at first surprised that Strong had recovered from the severe beating that he had inflicted on the youth, wasted no time in reaffirming his rights over his 'property'. Having no use for Strong himself anymore, Lisle negotiated terms to sell him to another Caribbean planter, James Kerr, who intended to purchase the former slave and ship him back to the West Indies. However, remembering the kindness expressed to him by his former mentor, Granville Sharp, Strong managed to get word to Sharp of his predicament.

Sharp seemed to be permanently a man of study and action. What he did not know, he learnt, and he was always ready to take up the case of some unfortunate soul who appeared to have been wronged. He made an intervention on behalf of Strong and appealed to the Lord Mayor to free him. The Lord Mayor agreed, but the situation was far from resolved as both Lisle and Kerr were grieved by the decision and decided to sue Sharp for loss of income and challenge him to a dual. Fortunately for Sharp, nothing came of either. However, the same could not be said of his charge, Jonathan Strong. Despite his surname, Strong never fully regained his robustness after his brutal beating, the stress of his arrest and the resulting legal proceedings, all of which took a toll on his health. He died aged just 25 in 1770.

There is little doubt that the Strong case helped Granville Sharpe discover his true vocation in life. Sharp is now recognized as the 'godfather' of the British abolition movement: he was fighting the cause of African freedom when Wilberforce and Clarkson were still in short trousers, Equiano was still in chains, Newton was still in denial about his role in the slave trade and Hannah More, whose poetry and prose would later lambaste the evils of the slave trade, was teaching girls to be prim and proper.

If one word could describe Granville Sharp it would have to be quirky. Born in Durham in 1735, Sharp decided against adopting the family career path of a clergyman – his father and grandfather were both Church of England vicars – and chose instead to apprentice himself to a linen draper in London. For someone possessing the ability to play numerous instruments, sing like a songbird and paint exquisitely, this career choice appeared particularly undemanding. As predicted, he soon tired of this profession and opted instead for a career in the civil service working as a clerk in the Ordinance Office. And yet this also failed to motivate him and after resigning from the Ordinance Office for political reasons, he occupied his time and energies writing letters to anyone who would listen to his views on such weighty subjects as constitutional reform, Mosaic Law and human rights.

Sharp was biding his time for something that could fully satisfy his great energies and the enormous battle to end slavery would meet that need. After the Jonathan Strong case, he spent most of his time and resources examining the status of slavery in England. In 1769, he produced *Representation of the injustice and dangerous tendency of admitting the least claim of private property in the persons of men in England, etc*, a tract that explored the rights of property against those of liberty in England. He also gained a reputation as the champion of Africans in England and was sought out by many an African runaway for his legal expertise and commitment to freedom.

One such African was James Somerset, a runaway living in London who arrived at Sharp's door in 1772 with a tale of woe. Somerset had accompanied his master, Charles Stewart, to Britain from Virginia in 1769. Upset with his life as a slave there, he absconded in late 1771 and lived among London's growing African population as a free man. The canny Stewart vigorously pursued his runaway, recapturing the hapless Somerset just a few months later. He subsequently made plans to transport the African to the warmer, slave-supporting environment of Jamaica.

A legal tussle pursued with Somerset imprisoned while the decision on his future waited to be settled. Just prior to the trial date he was freed and, like most in his position, made a beeline for Sharp's house. Sharp, for his part, had been looking for a case that would draw upon the legal expertise he had been amassing.

Presiding over the case was the venerable William Murray, better known as Lord Chief Justice Mansfield. Lord Mansfield, who was the leading lawyer of his day, was conservative minded but was also a fiercely independent individual who prided himself on his personal and professional integrity. In many respects, he was the ideal candidate for such a landmark case because West Indian planters, well aware that they could incur financial losses if all enslaved Africans were freed, would use any means necessary – including bribery – to get their way. Similarly, Sharp lived up to his name and used all manner of legal documents and persuasive arguments to plead a case not only for Somerset, but also for countless other Africans in similar positions.

After much dithering, the usually decisive Lord Mansfield delivered his judgment, which although it appeared clear, was nevertheless misinterpreted by many. Prefacing his judgment with the now infamous line, 'Let Justice be done, though the Heavens may fall', he went on to state that England's laws did not permit slave owner Charles Stewart the right to apprehend and transport James Somerset back overseas. And although many British colonies had laws supporting slavery, England did not. He wound up the case by stating, 'No master ever was allowed here to take a slave by force to be sold abroad because he deserted from his service… and therefore the man must be discharged.'

This was an obvious victory for Sharp and Somerset, and a careful reading of the ruling suggested that under English law – the law only applied to England – no runaway slave could be forced back into overseas slavery. What appears to have been a straightforward decision, however, was nevertheless interpreted by some as the ending of slavery in England to the extent that every slave who put his feet on English soil would automatically be free. Although the case did not strictly guarantee freedom, it generated tremendous interest in the issue of slavery throughout the country. It appeared also to highlight England's inconsistency over the rights of 'free born' Britons and her fondness for enslavement overseas. The growing number of abolitionists would take heart from Mansfield's decision and the higher profile of the anti-slavery campaign.

7

The Tide is Turning

Despite the great publicity surrounding the Somerset case of 1772 and the status and plight of enslaved Africans at home and abroad, Britain had to wait until 1783 for her first significant anti-slavery movement. The decade's expanse witnessed two events that profoundly influenced the abolition movement – the American War of Independence in the mid 1770s and the disastrous events on board the British slaver the *Zong* in 1781.

The American Revolution pitted American colonies against their colonial British masters. Never slow to turn an apparent disadvantage into an obvious advantage, Britain offered freedom to the enslaved Africans living in North America if they joined their side in the war. The Africans readily took up this altruistic – albeit opportunistic – offer and deserted North American plantations in droves to enlist. As it was, Britain subsequently lost the war, but felt duty-bound to honour the offer of freedom extended to the enlisted Africans. Britain eventually resettled the Africans in the chilly climes of Nova Scotia, and this scheme would subsequently form part of the Sierra Leone resettlement project championed by Granville Sharp and his colleagues and endorsed by Olaudah Equiano.

The *Zong* incident characterized the callous and calculating nature of the slave trade and the blatant disregard in which it held African lives. The *Zong* was a Liverpool-registered slaver which set sail from West Africa to Jamaica with its consignment of enslaved Africans in early September 1781. Luke Collingwood, the captain of the vessel, followed the usual practice of overloading the ship with Africans in order to maximize profits. With a financial stake in the venture, Collingwood stood to get a share of the profits when the ship docked in Jamaica. Unfortunately, early into the journey his greed and recklessness took a physical toll on both sailors and Africans alike, and by late November almost 70 were declared dead and many more were unwell. With one eye on his financial stake, Collingwood decided to jettison all sick Africans overboard. He knew that an insurance claim could be made if it could be proved that such an action was done for the safety of the ship and its remaining 'cargo'. He also knew that insurance laws governing the shipping industry declared that no claim could be made for natural death.

Consequently, Collingwood informed his crew that the water supply was running low and he gave orders to ditch every unwell African overboard. His crew, with the exception of the sailor James Kelsall, duly obliged and over 50 Africans headed to a watery grave. Emboldened by his previous day's activity, the following day he gave orders for a further 40 to be disposed of in a similar manner. By the third day, the Africans who were ill and still aboard defied their ailments and put up a struggle, but even so, over 20 died. In all, 132 enslaved Africans perished in this singular act of brutality. When the ship finally limped into Jamaica a few days before Christmas, contrary to Collingwood's claims, the ship had over 400 gallons of water on board which was more than enough for a full shipload of passengers.

The *Zong* case came to court in March 1783, not as a murder trial but as an insurance claim which eventually found in favour of the plaintiffs, Messrs Gregson, Collingwood and co. The case would have been confined to maritime insurance history had it not been for the keen eye of Olaudah Equiano, who having spotted the item in a daily newspaper, brought it to the attention of Granville Sharp. Equiano stands tall among the abolitionists of his day and explodes the myth that all abolitionists were white, well-to-do gentleman. He also invalidates the theory that Africans, if they were involved in the fight for freedom, preferred the machete or musket to the quill or pen. Equiano's story is instead one of courage, ingenuity and providence.

According to Equiano, he was born in what is now Nigeria around 1745. His life was uneventful until, aged 11, both he and his sister became victims of the growing slave trade in West Africa.[1] After six months of captivity in his homeland, Equiano was transported to Barbados where, after a brief stay, he was shipped to the then British colony of Virginia. While in North America, a British naval officer, Henry Pascal, purchased Equiano and renamed the young boy Gustavus Vassa. When Captain Pascal decided to return home to Britain, he took Equiano with him, thus giving the young African the experience of two-thirds of triangular enslavement within the space of just a few years.

While in London, Equiano stayed with Pascal's relatives and, most importantly, learnt to read and write. It is important to note that Equiano joined the growing numbers of African children consigned to the chambers and boudoirs of the wealthy. During the eighteenth century, it became the norm for wealthy West Indian planters and traders to return to Britain with their enslaved Africans in tow. These enslaved individuals, many of whom were very young, were a symbol of affluence and status and were often treated as a family pet rather than a member of the family.

Captain Pascal was a navy commander, and Equiano

accompanied him on various naval duties to Canada and Europe during the Seven Years' War with France. But after the war ended in 1763, Equiano was not only swindled out of the naval salary that he had been receiving, but was also sold. His new owner, James Doran, a sea captain, took Equiano to Montserrat. While there, Equiano witnessed the cruelty of plantation slavery, but thankfully was not forced to work on a plantation himself. Like most enslaved Africans, however, Equiano's life was at the whim of financially craven owners and he was sold again, this time to the Quaker merchant, Robert King. King quickly became aware of Equiano's intelligence, and was enlightened enough to grant him training in seafaring.

Historical studies demonstrate that most enslaved Africans sought freedom in a variety of ways, and Equiano was no exception. Over the next three years, he used his ingenuity and charm to save up the £40 required to buy his freedom from King in 1766. However, as a free person in the Americas, Equiano was aware of the limited career choices open to Africans and the threat of being sold back into slavery, so he took his chances and set sail for Britain. In 1767 he found work as a hairdresser in Coventry Court, Haymarket, London.

The following year, Dr Charles Irving, who was well known for his successful experiments in making fresh water from seawater, employed him. In between bouts at sea and exploring the North Pole, Equiano took a keen interest in the conditions of his fellow Africans in London, many of whom were living on the capital's streets having fled the cruelty of their masters, living a cloak-and-dagger existence in order to avoid recapture.

One of the earliest examples of Equiano's involvement in abolition activities occurred in 1773 when he intervened in the plight of the ex-enslaved African, John Annis. Annis was a cook on board a vessel moored on the Thames in London. His former owner, a disgruntled St Kitts merchant, planned to ship him back to the West Indies but when Equiano got wind of these plans, he confronted the merchant at his London residence to demand that he give up ownership over Annis. He also enlisted the services of Granville Sharp, whose legal interventions had outlawed the practice of the forced removal of slaves the previous year through the landmark Somerset case. However, Sharp could not work his magic for Annis, as he had done previously for Somerset, and the cook was forced back into a life of slavery.

Equiano became one of a group of Africans who worked with white abolitionists on various slave-related cases. He went on to form the Sons of Africa, a group that also included Quobna Ottobah Cugoano, which carried out letter-writing campaigns, public speaking and the lobbying of parliament. Equiano is perhaps best known, however, for his book *Interesting Narrative*, an autobiographical account of his life as both an enslaved African and a free-person. The book became a best seller in Britain and overseas (Germany and North America), and Equiano travelled around the country promoting his work and speaking against the injustices of the slave trade. The great evangelical leader John Wesley read the book on his deathbed in 1791, and as a result wrote his final letter to Wilberforce urging him to do all he could to end the slave trade.

When Equiano told Granville Sharp of the events of the *Zong*, Sharp brought this horrific case to the attention of the upper echelons of British society. Sharp also appealed the case before the familiar Lord Mansfield. Fired up with evangelical zeal, Sharp pointed out the barbarity of Collingwood's actions. He argued that the investors in the *Zong* should not have been compensated because there was no justification for jettisoning the enslaved Africans. Moreover, he added that the initial case should have been a murder trial rather than merely a compensation case. Despite his intervention, Sharp was unsuccessful in securing a prosecution; yet the involvement of Sharp and Equiano made a significant section of British society aware for the first time of the brutality of the slave trade.

The *Zong* affair also acted as a catalyst for sustained anti-slave activity. That same year, 1783, British Quakers formed an anti-slavery committee in order to agitate against slavery and the slave trade. Although still a relatively small denomination in Britain, the Quakers were nevertheless a well-organized, highly efficient group. Similarly, a century's worth of ostracism from society due to their stance on various political and religious matters had taught the Quakers how to be economically self-sufficient. In the 1780s, Quakers owned numerous businesses in a variety of professions which provided them with the financial means to carry out anti-slavery activities on both sides of the Atlantic. According to the historian Christopher Hill, the Quakers 'evolved a group loyalty in the dark days of persecution in the later seventeenth century. They were likely to deposit their money within a family or sectarian group'.[2]

In Britain, the Quakers owned printers and publishing houses which enabled them to circulate a range of material to local Quaker Meeting Houses, highlighting both the plight of Africans in Africa and the Americas, and current activities taking place to fight this. James Phillips, who owned an influential Quaker-run publishing company and would be a founder member of the Committee for the Abolition of the African Slave Trade (later the Society for the Abolition of the Slave Trade) in 1787, disseminated the anti-slavery pamphlets of Anthony Benezet and Revd James Ramsay. The Quakers had found a useful ally in the Church of England vicar, Ramsay. He had first-hand knowledge of the slave trade having been a ship's doctor on board a slaver, where he witnessed the degradations and brutality of the trade while ministering to both sick Africans and crewmen. Appalled by what he saw, Ramsay resigned his post and became a clergyman on the West Indian island of St Kitts.

Ramsay's evangelical brand of Christianity brought him immediately into conflict with West Indian planters who were appalled that he insisted on racially integrating his religious services. He also carried out missionary activities among enslaved Africans, which brought him into further conflict with the white West Indian authorities. The planters were always suspicious of any social action among Africans and they quickly turned against Ramsay, accusing him of everything from seditious preaching to serial philandering. Such was the level of opposition that Ramsay was forced to abandon the West Indies in the 1780s, a man broken by the relentless lies and misinformation of those who had taken exception to his hard work among Africans.

Ramsay recorded his opinions on slavery in the Quaker-published *Essay on the Treatment Conversion of the African slaves in the British Sugar Colonies*, where he described the average day of an enslaved African on a plantation as follows: '... at four o'clock in the morning the plantation bell rings to call the slaves into the field... About nine o'clock they have half an hour for breakfast, which they take into the field. Again they fall to work... until eleven o'clock or noon; the bell rings and the slaves are dispersed in the neighbourhood to pick up natural grass and weeds for the horses and cattle (and to prepare and eat their own lunch)... At one, or in some plantations at two o'clock, the bell summons them to deliver in... their grass and assemble fieldwork... About half an hour before sunset they are again required to collect grass – about seven o'clock in the evening or later according to season – deliver grass as before then dismissed to return to their huts, picking up brushwood or dry cow dung to prepare supper and tomorrow's breakfast. They go to sleep at about midnight.'³

Ramsay's activities helped to stir many in the church and he used his time in Britain to work on behalf of the Quaker-led anti-slavery lobby. He died in 1789, never fully recovering from his West Indian experiences. On hearing of his death, a West Indian planter named Molyneux allegedly boasted, 'Ramsay is dead – I have killed him.'

Ramsay was unlike many Christian ministers in the West Indies. Prior to the evangelical revival in Britain in the second half of the eighteenth century, the average British clergyman often had to be dragged kicking and screaming to the West Indies. West Indian society was often a wanton place that cared more for carousing and violence than organized religion; very few, from the king's representative down to the lowly peasant, took Christian teachings seriously in a society built on slavery and shaped largely on inequality, exploitation and discrimination.

Those living in the West Indies had little interest in following teachings that would possibly criticize the way that their society was governed. As a result, clergymen faced several choices: maintain their integrity and carry out their work regardless; adapt their message to suit their new environment or abandon their clerical duties altogether. Because of this, some clergymen and missionaries argued that Christianity was compatible with slavery and that it was possible for Africans to be both good Christians and slaves at the same time. Indeed, prior to embarking on his missionary activities in Demerara (modern-day Guyana), the London Missionary Society told Revd John Smith that, 'Not a word must escape you in public or private

151

which might render the slaves displeased with their masters or dissatisfied with their station. You are sent not to relieve them from their servile condition, but to afford them the consolation of religion'.[4]

The more conscientious, but equally cowardly, clergymen cautioned West Indian planters and estate managers on the liberal use of the whip on their enslaved Africans, especially on women and children. Others used the Bible to implore slave owners to treat their enslaved Africans fairly. 'Do not threaten them, since you know that he who is both their master and yours is in heaven, and there is no favouritism with him',[5] ensuring that the Bible was used to attack the excesses of slavery if not the system itself.

Apart from their clerical attire, the behaviour of some British clergymen was often indistinguishable from that of the West Indian planters. Many were corrupted by West Indian society to such an extent that they spent more time attending extravagant social functions than being in church. It was also not unknown for clergymen to be in possession of enslaved Africans or to help planters with their work. Perhaps the clearest example of the cosy relationship between religion and West Indian slavery occurred on the island of Barbados in the early part of the eighteenth century.

In 1710, Sir Christopher Codrington died. Oxford educated and captain-general of the Leeward Isles, he had amassed a vast fortune from sugar plantations in the West Indies and left some of these to the Church of England's Society for the Propagation of the Gospel (now USPG) on his death. The Society ran these plantations with great aplomb, with the Bishop of London acting as their CEO and other senior clergy carrying out important duties such as determining how and where profits should be invested. (In February 2006, the Church of England

General Synod examined its role during the time of West Indian slavery, with a particular emphasis on its ownership of the Codrington Estate in Barbados. The Archbishop of Canterbury, Rowan Williams, offered an 'apology' for the church's involvement in the owning and exploitation of Africans.)

It would be very easy to pass judgment on these so-called men of God for their moral failings; however, any criticism must be tempered with the realization that they were living in debased societies where violence and terror held sway. Clergymen who preached that Africans were 'brothers and sisters in the Lord' or that they were also 'made in the image of God' were regarded as either dangerous or insane, or both. Equally, clergy who urged planters to be more compassionate towards their Africans were verbally or physically threatened, and in some instances run out of the West Indies on trumped-up charges.

The lot of the clergyman or missionary was rarely a happy one during the time of West Indian slavery. Life was a balance between obeying one's calling to preach the Christian message, and obeying the strict rules and regulations of the colonial authorities and planters to avoid teaching Africans anything that they could use to challenge the system. Most whites in the West Indies feared that Africans would interpret certain scriptural verses to argue that the Bible condemned slavery and upheld their right to freedom. They also discouraged Africans from reading and writing because this was regarded as equally subversive and could lead to Africans using these skills to be informed and educated about slavery and freedom issues. The Governor of Martinique spoke for many when he said, 'Religious instruction could give these Negroes here an opening to other knowledge, to a kind of reason... The safety of the whites, fewer in number, surrounded by these people on their estates, and at their mercy, demands that they are kept in the profoundest ignorance.'[6] It is ironic that practically all the major African uprisings were religiously inspired and led by literate Africans.

While many of the whites in the West Indies could be described as cultural rather than practising Christians, they nevertheless regarded themselves as Christians. They did not like the idea of worshipping in the same churches as Africans or sharing the same pews as their enslaved Africans. On a deeper level, any scriptural teachings that argued that Africans could be Christians also questioned a slave owner's right to treat them unfairly.

Planters and estate managers were well known for their callousness, a disposition that summed up the brutality of plantation slavery and slave society generally. They believed that violence was central to the successful functioning of a plantation and they did not want to sit through sermons on 'brotherly love' or curtailing their chastisement of stubborn slaves. As far as they were concerned, Africans were similar to children and they believed that the Bible advocated punishing children.

It would be no exaggeration to suggest that slave-based society in the West Indies displayed such an aversion to Christianity that it is possible to compare it to modern-day countries that persecute religious believers. Developed in such as way as to undermine organized religion, ethical values were pitted against economic considerations. Sometimes this conflict was played out subtly but at other times it was more overt. An example of the subtle ways in which slave-based society clashed with Christianity can be seen in the work regime of enslaved Africans in many parts of the West Indies. Africans usually worked six days a week and were allowed to rest on the

Sabbath, but many chose – or were encouraged – to grow foodstuffs in order to supplement their meagre diets as, despite working exceedingly hard on the plantation, the diets of the enslaved African were far from nutritious and often lacked vegetables.

Africans were also keen to cultivate produce because any food surpluses could be sold at the market and any money accrued saved up to purchase their freedom. Slavery in the Americas always held out the often-illusive promise of freedom for Africans, if they could obtain the necessary funds to purchase it. Some, such as Olaudah Equiano, managed to buy their way out of slavery, but most Africans were less fortunate as slave-based societies had a vested interest in maintaining the status of Africans. Consequently, Sunday in most parts of the British West Indies usually saw Africans attending provision grounds or markets rather than going to church.

Economic forces would also triumph over religion when it came to harvesting the ripe sugarcane, which took over a year to grow but had to be harvested in a few days. Crop time was always a stressful period as the whole plantation worked to bring in the harvest. It was all systems go and nothing was allowed to get in the way – not even a religious service or an act of worship. The only Africans attending church during crop time were the old or the lame as everyone else was busy turning the sugarcane into money. If the crop failed or was spoilt, the whole plantation would be bankrupted.

The clash between God and mammon was also a feature of the other non-English-speaking islands. The eminent Cuban historian Manuel Moreno Fraginals points to an African rebellion on the Spanish-run island of Cuba, caused by the clash between religion and money. According to Fraginals, during one particular Holy Week in Cuba, the Count de Casa Bayona, a pious, wealthy sugar planter from the south-east of the island, selected a dozen of his Africans to recreate the Last Supper of Jesus and his disciples. During the course of the meal, the count likened himself to Jesus and extolled the virtues of Christianity to his enslaved Africans, whom he chose to call his disciples. The Africans questioned him on a number of religious matters and by the end of the meal, the now almost paralytic count promised to allow the twelve 'time off' work in honour of the 'Saviour who died for all'. Unfortunately, Easter that year was too close to harvest and his overseer and accountant were forced to remind the now sober count of his drunken folly. The twelve Africans were consequently roused from their Easter rest and told to labour on one of the holiest days in the Christian calendar. They naturally took umbrage at the count's hypocrisy, burnt down the plantation and fled. Full of anger, the count hunted down his former disciples and captured and killed eleven of them. Ironically, the one African who refused to pay any attention to the count's pontificating during the meal was the only one not re-captured during the hunt.

The role of the church during slavery was often that of a passive observer or bystander who 'held the coats while a stoning took place'. There are accounts of a clergyman in Jamaica who tried to conduct a Sunday morning service while enslaved Africans were being flogged outside. The noise of the whips on the Africans' flesh, and their resultant screaming, could even be heard above the musical accompaniment. Worried that the noise was disturbing the sanctity of his service, the clergyman ordered the overseer to halt the punishment until the service had ended.

This attitude was by no means the exception in the West Indies. Far too few clergymen had the attitude of James Ramsay and instead condoned laws that banned Africans from having religious acts of worship between sunset and sunrise during weekdays. Others failed to complain at regulations that forced clerics in some West Indian islands to apply for licences in order to preach the gospel. So Ramsay stands like a towering giant among pygmies and there is little doubt that his work among enslaved Africans influenced another giant of the abolition movement, Thomas Clarkson.

It can be argued that no one travelled farther, gathered more evidence or spoke to more people about anti-slavery activities than Thomas Clarkson. Of all the abolitionists, he appeared the most consistent and, by today's highly critical standards of leadership, he is the one with the least foibles. There is little doubt that the abolitionists, as men and women of their time, rightly have their detractors. Granville Sharp was an unconventional man, whose eccentricities increased with age. At times, he appeared to show greater charity towards enslaved Africans living overseas than British Catholics and argued against Catholic entry into Sierra Leone during the early years of the province's relocation scheme. William Wilberforce was conservative in every sense of the word and his zeal to end slavery never matched his desire to end the actual Transatlantic Slave Trade.

According to the writers Terence Brady and Evan Jones, '[Wilberforce]... disassociated himself from any notion of emancipation until the slaves were properly prepared for it, declaring himself and his colleagues as "satisfied with having gained an object [the ending of the slave trade] which is safely attainable".'[7] The writers argue that, because of this disinterest, Africans were condemned to 'another 30 years of penal captivity'.

Equiano, the one-time enslaved African, thought nothing of buying slaves himself and forcing them to work on plantations in Central America, and John Newton, who became a Christian in 1748, continued his involvement in slave trading until 1754, when poor health rather than moral compunction forced him to withdraw from the profession. He continued to live off his investments in the slave trade after his retirement until he ran into financial difficulties. It would take the great man several decades to speak out against the horrors in which he had participated.

The most that can be levelled against Clarkson, however, is the accusation of self-righteousness and being a trifle smug. His views on the emancipation question were well ahead of his rivals and, according to the historian Eric Williams, who was no fan of Christian-based philanthropy, Clarkson 'was one of those friends of whom the Negro race has had unfortunately only too few'.[8]

Thomas Clarkson was born in Wisbech, Cambridgeshire in 1760, and, like Granville Sharp, decided against following in his father's footsteps by becoming a clergyman. Clarkson's father died when he was only six, and young Thomas, a very capable student, won a scholarship to St John's College, Cambridge for the offspring of dead clergy.

Two events led to Clarkson's involvement in the anti-slavery campaign. First, he entered a Cambridge University essay contest in 1785, which he won with the paper *Is it licit to make slaves of others against their will?* Clarkson's paper on slavery relied heavily on the work of Anthony Benezet, and his prize whetted his appetite to discover more about the slave trade. Reflecting on his prize-winning essay he wrote, 'It was but one gloomy subject from morning to night. I sometimes never closed my eyelids for grief. It became now not so much a trial for academic reputation as for the production of a work which might be useful to injured Africa.'[9]

The second key event occurred shortly after winning his

esteemed prize. While making his way to London on horseback, he became absorbed by many of the points that he had examined in his essay. He dismounted his horse and had an epiphany moment regarding the anti-slavery campaign. After a period of reflection, this new convert to the anti-slavery cause searched for fellow believers, whom he quickly found in the form of Granville Sharp and the Quakers.

There is little doubt that Clarkson's involvement with the fledgling anti-slavery movement was mutually beneficial. In Clarkson, the anti-slavery movement had a young man with boundless energy, great intelligence and, as history would reveal, real courage. Clarkson, on the other hand, received from his compatriots the opportunity to familiarize himself with others working to end slavery. The Quakers would also publish his essay in 1786 after it was translated from Latin into English.

Aware that they had made little real headway in their anti-slavery pamphleteering, the Quakers made the move to broaden the religious focus of their committee and invited the Church of England members Ramsay, Sharp and Clarkson to help form a new anti-slavery committee of 12 men in May 1787. Called the Committee for the Abolition of the African Slave Trade (later the Society for the Abolition of the Slave Trade) and with Sharp as its Chair, the Quaker-dominated committee held its meetings in a backroom of the Phillips bookstore in London where they discussed everything from the morality of slave trading to 'legitimate' forms of commerce with Africa.

Unlike its predecessor, this committee was born of pragmatism and nourished on common sense. Members agreed that although slavery was abhorrent, its first task was to end the actual slave trade. They believed that once people were supplied with the full facts about the trade's brutality, the country would quickly move against it.

It is easy to denounce this approach as naive, especially when committee members asserted that, by cutting off the pool of enslaved Africans, West Indian planters would be forced to treat those remaining in their care with more compassion. Critics have since suggested, however, that this approach is evidence of the abolitionists having little interest in liberating Africans due to a paternalistic attitude that believed Africans incapable of running their own affairs. This mindset encouraged amelioration – the gradual improvement of conditions on plantations such as the removal of terror and violence, and offering a more humane treatment. But although not every committee member shared this short-sighted belief in African competence, nearly all preferred African 'improvement' to self-determination, and the Sierra Leone Project was evidence of this.

The Sierra Leone scheme involved several abolition committee members, including Granville Sharp, who drew up plans to return Africans in London to the West African colony of Sierra Leone. Europeans would work with Africans to run the colony, but overall control would rest with white hands in London, rather than black hands in Sierra Leone. Many of the Africans in question were ex-slaves or runaways who were to be found languishing in dire poverty on London's streets. In 1787, ships set sail for Africa with over 400 Africans and hundreds of white prostitutes and other women of ill repute.

The population of Sierra Leone was further swelled by 1,000 African-Americans who had fought with the British against their American masters during the War of Independence. It was a testimony to British integrity that such Africans were not abandoned to face the retribution of the white North American patriots they had fought against. Their reward for fighting on the losing side was residency in the cold climes of Nova Scotia, but local African-rights agitators such as Thomas Peters put pressure on Britain to find a permanent residence for the Africans. Peters travelled to Britain and met with Granville Sharp. It seemed logical to all concerned that Sierra Leone was the appropriate place for resettlement as the Africans needed a permanent residence and Sierra Leone needed residents. Peters successfully petitioned the British government to grant free passage to Sierra Leone for the growing number of Africans on Nova Scotia. The man chosen to take the Africans on this sea-bound journey to the African 'Promised Land' was John Clarkson, Thomas Clarkson's younger brother.

According to Simon Schama, it was 'Clarkson's willingness to listen, his openness to change his mind and his good faith and transparent affections towards them [Africans] that won the blacks' respect as no other white Briton, with the exception of Granville Sharp, ever did.'[10] Clarkson the younger had served in the American War of Independence and journeyed to Nova Scotia and, with Peters' assistance, made arrangements for the mass exodus. The 15 ships left Halifax harbour in January 1792 and arrived in Sierra Leone several weeks later.

The Nova Scotia Africans would have been taken aback by Sierra Leone's almost utopian-like concepts. The colony was basically the concern of the Sierra Leone Company, in which Sharp, Clarkson and numerous other evangelical Christian abolitionists held shares. As a consequence, it was run on Christian values, promoted freedom (the capital was called Freetown) and championed non-slave related ('legitimate') trade commerce practices with outsiders. But the dilemma that local dwellers faced was that the slave-trading industry continued to dominate the economies of the neighbouring kingdoms, which made it difficult to sell or purchase items to or from bordering states without colluding in some way with the slave trade.

The residents also struggled to come to terms with the weather conditions, which played havoc with harvests and made life generally miserable. They battled droughts and floods, many crops were destroyed by infestations, and diseases such as yellow fever and dysentery accounted for many deaths. To make matters worse, the French, who were still involved in the slave trade, attacked the colony with particular venom on at least one occasion.

The main criticism of the Sierra Leone scheme was that it failed to make appropriate use of the Africans who would resettle in the colony. The likes of Equiano, who had been encouraged to sell the scheme to his African brethren, and Thomas Peters, whom the historian Simon Schama describes as the 'first true African American politician' were accorded only bit parts within the project. Many of the Africans involved were educated, capable individuals who had used skill, courage and perseverance to buy their way out of slavery. And yet they had to stand by while a range of British-appointed governors of mixed ability, including the leading abolitionists Zachary Macaulay and Dr Alexander Falconbridge, ran the colony on their behalf.

For the evangelicals whose brainchild the project was, Sierra Leone carried almost biblical connotations. Some compared the Africans to the Hebrews in the Old Testament, who were captured and taken to Babylon where they were kept in bondage. Sierra Leone represented an end to African bondage and exile – the 'modern-day Hebrews' would be free in their 'New Jerusalem'. Unfortunately for the British, many of the Africans wanted a Moses-type figure who looked like them and who had their best interests at heart, and Thomas Peters naturally fitted the bill. His supporters put his name forward, but Peters died before the matter came to a head.

Although the Africans were fairly treated and had opportunities to voice their opinions about how the colony was being run, they were denied real power to make the changes that were required to turn the colony into a success. They were especially frustrated over issues of land and taxes. Granville Sharp and his colleagues back in London suggested that tax was proportionate to the size of the land and that a levy should also be charged on any produce grown on the land. This cemented the feeling among many African settlers that the Sierra Leone Company was not acting in their best interests but instead looking to cover its costs.

Some detractors have since denounced the Sierra Leone project as repatriation by another name. It has been seen as a high-minded yet hypocritical way of ridding the country of its rising black population. The eighteenth century was an era in which Britain was looking to offload those deemed surplus to requirements, with the West Indies and newer territories such as Australia largely being the recipients of this policy. Some in Britain wanted Africans to leave because they feared they were corrupting the virtues of the country's white women, while others were tired of seeing them reduced to begging on London streets. Such were the numbers of destitute Africans in the country that Jonas Hanway helped to establish the Committee for the Relief of the Black Poor in the mid 1780s.

According to Simon Schama, the harsh winter of 1785–86 was one of the factors that encouraged Hanway to do something for the numerous Africans living in poverty. 'In the East End and Rotherhithe: tattered bundles of human misery, huddled in doorways, shoeless, sometimes shirtless even in the bitter cold or else covered with filthy rags.'[11]

The committee met to find answers to the plight of the destitute. Their usual answer involved handing out food, which they bought with money donated by committee members. Members of the committee moved in high circles and they managed to get the government to contribute towards their work. Nevertheless, the government at that time had no wish to develop a welfare state approach to the upkeep of Africans, nor did the committee members have the resources to sustain their generosity *ad infinitum*. The obvious solution would, therefore, have been to 'send them home'.

Additionally, there was also a historical precedent for Britain trying to rid herself of its unwanted black population. On 11 July 1596, Queen Elizabeth I sent an open letter to the Lord Mayor of London and his alderman, and to the mayors and sheriffs of the other towns to rid London and other cities of their rising population in 'blackamoores'. Five years later she dispatched the following declaration, stating that she was 'highly discontented to understand the great numbers of negars and Blackamoores which... are crept into this realm... who are fostered and relieved here to the great annoyance of her own people...'.[12]

The Sierra Leone experiment has also been described as a forerunner to the colonialism that would take place in Africa later in the nineteenth century, when Africa would receive British religious, cultural and political ideas to enlighten the continent. This acculturation became known as as the three 'Cs': Christianity, Commerce and Civilization – 'partners in the advancement of what were seen as backward peoples'.[13]

The Committee for the Abolition of the African Slave Trade regarded the Sierra Leone project as a worthy scheme to help displaced, free Africans, but they knew that the real work had to be carried out among those still in chains. Their work up until then had largely involved leafleting, public speaking and gentle persuasion, and yet appealing to the hearts and minds of the great British public would not bring about the end of the slave trade. The committee members knew that they needed an outstanding representative in parliament who could present their case among the real decision-makers in the land. Such a man was hard to find. This was the era of patronage in which wealth and land equated to automatic power; no one had more money or influence than West Indian planters and many absentee planters ended up in parliament. They used their seats in the House of Commons to ensure that bills were passed to safeguard their slave-related interests. Moreover, slave trade propaganda argued that the country's economic fortunes were inextricably linked to the trade and its related concerns in the Caribbean. Only someone extremely brave – or foolhardy – would challenge such vested interests and so the committee turned its attentions to a young, articulate MP named William Wilberforce.

Wilberforce is now regarded as Hull's favourite son. His influence permeates every section of the city and his name is immortalized in university departments (the Wilberforce Institute for the Study of Slavery and Emancipation) and museums (Wilberforce House) as well as on various statues and plaques. Indeed plans to commemorate the bicentenary of the abolition of the slave trade act in Hull were given the imaginative title of Wilberforce 2007. But interestingly, the great man spent less than a quarter of his life in the city. Indeed, such is the stature of Wilberforce that many places with even less of a connection to him than Hull lay claim to him, such as Clapham, Mill Hill and Kensington.

William Wilberforce was born on 24 August 1759 in High Street, Hull and baptized a month later at Holy Trinity Church. His grandfather, a wealthy merchant from the Baltic trade, became a leading figure in Hull, rising to the rank of alderman and Mayor of Hull. His father Robert, who was born in 1728, joined the family business, rising to become a partner in the firm. The Hull of Wilberforce's youth was centred around the port and the Baltic trade. He attended Hull Grammar School; however, following the death of his father in 1768, he was sent to live with his uncle, also called William, in London.

Wilberforce's uncle and aunt were fervent evangelical Christians who cleaved to the religious teachings of George Whitefield and John Wesley, creating problems for the more traditional members of the Wilberforce family. His family in Hull soon became so concerned about this religious influence that they took him back to his native Hull in 1771, where they enrolled him in Pocklington Grammar School. He then attended St John's College, Cambridge, in 1776, like his colleague Thomas Clarkson. Unlike Clarkson, however, his time at the university was not distinguished by essay winning, but instead by entertaining, socializing, attending balls and visiting friends.

He left university in 1779 and chose to enter politics rather than the thriving family business. There Wilberforce became friends with William Pitt, who was later to become prime minister – like his father before him. Pitt the Younger, as he was known, was born in the same year as Wilberforce and had also attended Cambridge University. Pitt urged Wilberforce to stand as an MP in his hometown of Hull, which he did and duly won the seat in September 1780. His victory was undoubtedly due to a combination of his charm, youth and excellent oratory skills. A further factor was probably his family's wealth, which enabled him to purchase the necessary votes.

The parliamentary system at that time allowed only around 10 per cent of men the right to vote and these individuals tended to be landed gentry or those with money. However, 'freemen' were also allowed to vote and any man could join this category by virtue of inheritance, purchase or apprenticeship. Being a freeman proved especially lucrative around election time when potential MPs would buy their votes for around two guineas a time. This rather shady system was one of the primary means by which many became parliamentarians and it cost Wilberforce around £8,000 (roughly £760,000 today) to obtain his seat. Many years later, Wilberforce would work to outlaw this, considering it to be a dishonest system. His tenure as MP for Hull lasted a mere four years, however, and by 1 April 1784 he had switched seats to become one of the two county members for Yorkshire.

Political seat changes aside, the real transformation in Wilberforce's life occurred in 1785 when he became what his mother had dreaded, a fervent evangelical Christian. Indeed, such was the 'great change', as he described it, that he contemplated giving up politics for a life as a clergyman. Whether he would have exchanged parliament for the pulpit will never be known because John Newton, the one-time slave trader, persuaded Wilberforce that he could also serve God in parliament by improving standards within the House of Commons.

Wilberforce's conversion was followed by what is often the classic Christian renunciation of the former 'things of the flesh'. He resigned from all his clubs and societies and exchanged his socializing and entertaining for one of reflection and re-evaluation – although this put a real strain on his relationship with William Pitt, who was known for his love of a bottle or two of port.

Paintings of Wilberforce during his early parliamentary days show a man who could not be described by any stretch of the imagination as 'classically good looking'. He also lacked the physical presence of some of his political peers. But what he lacked in physical stature he more than made up for in character. He possessed masses of charm and a mesmerizing wit, and his trump card was his outstanding skill as a public speaker, which many of his peers compared to that of the great Greek orators. Added to this, his firm religious beliefs equipped him with a sense of destiny and resolve, and a strong moral code which could not be swayed by unscrupulous individuals who looked to 'buy' MPs. It was easy to see why the abolitionists wanted such a man to speak for their cause.

Consequently, in January 1887, Thomas Clarkson paid a visit to Wilberforce's Westminster home with the intention of persuading the MP to champion the anti-slavery cause in parliament. But although this is seen as an essential moment in the anti-slavery movement, Clarkson was no doubt only one of many abolitionists attempting to persuade Wilberforce to join the anti-slavery campaign.

His spiritual advisor was the former slave-trader-turned-clergyman, Revd John Newton, who was keen to do something to end the trade in which he had participated. Equally, David Hartley, who lost his seat to Wilberforce in Hull in 1780, had raised the slave trade question in parliament in 1776. And although Pitt was no longer a drinking partner, he remained a firm friend. Indeed, during the legendary conversation between the two men under an oak tree in Keston, a village on the outskirts of south-east London, Wilberforce resolved to end slavery.

The meeting between Clarkson and Wilberforce on that cold January day was one of contrasts: Clarkson stood over six feet tall while Wilberforce was a few inches over five feet; if both had attended St John's Cambridge, Clarkson was a prize-winning essayist whereas Wilberforce, by his own admission, was idle and failed to win an honours degree. On the other hand, Wilberforce was well connected and counted Prime Minister William Pitt as a close friend, while Clarkson was known only to a handful of abolitionists. What they did have in common, however, was a shared sense of passion – Clarkson had found his true vocation following the success of his prize-winning essay while Wilberforce at this point was looking for something to consume his tremendous energies.

With Wilberforce on board, the committee knew that it had found the last piece in the jigsaw. Through its Quaker connections, the committee had access to publishing and distributions networks and other wealthy benefactors were bankrolling its work. In Thomas Clarkson, the committee had what we would now call a 'chief researcher' who was responsible for gathering evidence of the full extent of the slave trade's barbarity and injustice to enslaved Africans. Clarkson approached this task with the efficiency of an accountant and the guile of a super sleuth. In fact, he did not have to look too far – or hard – for evidence of cruelty and injustice in cities such as Liverpool, London and Bristol.

Prior to setting off on the first of his numerous fact-finding journeys, Clarkson waxed lyrical about the task, even though he knew the forces that he was up against. Many people in Britain's slaving towns would see him as the enemy who, to mix a metaphor, was entering 'the lion's den in order to take away the golden egg-laying goose'. Although Clarkson could never be described as naive, only the brave – or foolhardy – would consider entering cities built on the slave trade in a bid to gather evidence to end the commerce. For this task, Clarkson's only aide was a pen, and it is hard to picture this young, well-spoken man traipsing through the docks, taverns and slave ships during the course of his investigations busily gathering information.

To say Clarkson was intrepid, however, would be an

understatement as he spoke to anyone who would speak to him about the slave trade. He obtained accounts from sailors who seemed to be permanently apprehensive of young Clarkson's motives; yet he managed to cajole a great many into giving first-hand accounts of the brutality of the slave trade. He spoke to doctors and surgeons who worked on slavers and was provided with appalling accounts of their work saving lives on board these vessels. His investigation took him all over the country and everything was put into his book. In Bristol and London, he came by all manner of contraptions used to punish or control Africans, and boarded slave ships to make measurements of the holds that stored the enslaved Africans.

Clarkson's activities did not go unnoticed by interested parties and he was often jostled and even attacked for his anti-slavery work. Once, while standing on Liverpool docks observing passing vessels, a mob attacked him, pushing him to the edge of the pier in order to throw him into the Mersey. According to Clarkson, 'I darted forward... One of them against whom I pushed myself, fell down. Their ranks were broken and I escaped, not without blows, amidst their implications and abuse.'[14] Clarkson would put his escape down to providence because, being unable to swim, he would surely have drowned. But if Clarkson was a *persona non-grata* around seaports, so was anyone with whom he associated. Sailors who provided him with evidence faced violent reprisals, ship doctors who gave him information were refused sea duties and merchants who cooperated with his investigations found their businesses shunned.

Clarkson remained undaunted by the threats, however, and continued travelling around the country on horseback, gathering material for his investigations. The more he looked, the more he found. He was stunned at the pervasiveness and perversity of Britain's deep involvement in the slave trade and his work in gathering evidence became his own personal crusade against a wicked system. It has been said that Clarkson and the abolitionists were the first to use tactics and methods that are now commonplace such as petitions, slogans, mottos and banners. They skilfully used what were undoubtedly propaganda tools to depict acts of singular barbarity as the norm. The West Indian sugar lobby in Britain, for example, frequently accused the abolitionists of exaggeration in their accounts of the horrors of the slave trade and West Indian plantation slavery. While it was true that Clarkson and his colleagues always preferred to portray individual cases of mass deaths on slave ships or the brutal flogging of enslaved Africans by a plantation overseer as truly representative of slavery, the West Indian sugar lobbyists chose to depict slavery as benign – or even beneficial – towards Africans.

As is the case today, the abolitionists knew that the British people would show a real interest in anti-slavery if a personal dimension to the suffering could be applied. Clarkson went out of his way to show that the slave trade was as detrimental to British life as it was to African, and that it was in the best interests of Britons and Africans alike that the slave trade be abolished. His research connected the high mortality rates among sailors to the heavy demands of the slave trade and pointed out that those who gathered at seaports to wave bon voyage to loved ones working on slave ships could be saying goodbye for ever.

Clarkson produced figures which showed that slave trading was so cruel and prejudicial to sailors that many chose to abscond rather than lose their lives at sea. Clarkson's research showed that in 1787, of the 88 ships that left Liverpool for Africa, 1,100 of the 3,170 crew deserted. Most importantly, Clarkson was one of the first people to believe that Africa could trade with Europe without the exchange of human beings. He firmly held the view that Africa had both the natural resources and skills to engage with Europe on mutually beneficial terms.

Clarkson normally travelled with a chest of African-sourced artefacts or 'exhibits' such as woven cloths, pepper, ivory, palm oil, rice, cinnamon and guinea-grass, which he believed could replace the slave trade as a more ethical and financially viable alternative. In 1788, Clarkson spoke about the contents of his chest to a Privy Council Inquiry on the slave trade where he explained that '… Africa was capable of affording instead of the Slave Trade, and that they might make a proper estimate of the… talents of the natives. The samples had been obtained by great labour at no inconsiderable expense…'.[15]

No matter how far Clarkson travelled, how many people he interviewed and how many hearts he managed to change, only parliament at the end of the day had the ability to ban the slave trade, and this was where Wilberforce's influence became critical. By late 1787, Wilberforce had begun his anti-slavery activities in parliament in earnest. He had contacted and received support from sympathetic MPs about his intention to introduce a motion on the subject of the slave trade in the next session of parliament. In a letter to a colleague around that time, he suggested, 'the cause of our poor Africans goes on most prosperously. I trust there is little reason to doubt of the motion for the abolition of this horrid traffic being carried out in parliament.'

In 1787, Wilberforce's good friend William Pitt had become prime minister, and Wilberforce spent his time persuading him to outlaw Britain's involvement in the trade. In fact, Pitt shared his colleague's desire to end the trade, but he also knew its financial worth and asked Wilberforce, 'would you not leave alone an enterprise on which the nation thrives?' By the late 1780s, Pitt also believed he had bigger concerns to deal with, such as Britain's socio-political and economic situation –

Britain's part in quelling the rebellion of the North American colonies during the American War of Independence had led to a national debt of staggering proportions.

Equally, Prime Minister Pitt had to grapple with the constitutional crisis caused by the illness of King George III, who was thought to be suffering from some form of mental disorder. (Doctors now agree that he fell victim to the blood disorder, porphyria, which was unknown at this time.) The disease had a debilitating effect on the king, and his apparent 'madness' had led to calls for a Regency or interim replacement. Fortunately for Pitt, the king recovered just after a Regency Bill had been introduced and passed in parliament. For all the political distractions, however, Wilberforce did manage to wrangle a concession from Pitt who instructed the Trade Committee of the Privy Council to conduct a year-long enquiry into the slave trade before then reporting back to him.

The former British Prime Minister Harold Macmillan allegedly used the words 'Events, dear boy, events' when responding to a question about what could easily steer a government or a politician off-course. The events of February 1788 not only steered Wilberforce off-course, they almost cost him his life. Wilberforce fell ill that month of an intestinal disorder and lay on his deathbed. It has been suggested that he was suffering from a case of ulcerative colitis, which is caused by stress. Wilberforce was never a robust man and his workload prior to his physical demise would have tested even the most vigorous of men. Convinced that he was not long for this world, Wilberforce persuaded Pitt to take up his abolition work when he died, but Pitt was spared this onerous duty when Wilberforce confounded his doctors – and himself – by recovering several weeks later. His doctor prescribed opium, which was commonly recommended for intestinal complaints and was deemed a legitimate medicine at the time.

However, Wilberforce continued to take doses in pill form for the rest of his life, leading to suggestions that he may have been addicted to the opiate. There are no suggestions though that the opium impaired his overall judgment or affected his ability to perform as an MP, and he continued his tireless work to end the trade.

By May 1788, Pitt proposed that the House of Commons should investigate the slave trade, a debate that would take place after the Privy Council reported back the following year. When it eventually arrived, the report proved a real revelation for all concerned. Steering clear of moral judgments on the slave trade, it purported to present the 'facts' about all aspects of the trade. This included descriptions of Africans as 'people devoid of morals and religion', who for the most part had been slaves in their own countries prior to becoming enslaved elsewhere. The report also contained evidence from supporters and detractors of the slave trade. The supporters gave evidence that the trade was humane and saved Africans from savagery in their homelands. Conversely, the evidence from the detractors gave a more balanced account of events.

Wilberforce, now fully recovered from his illness, used the Privy Council report to make his first major abolition speech in the House of Commons on 12 May 1789. He was a noted orator with very few equals in the House at that time. His three-hour address combined pathos with moral indignation as, point-by-point, he demolished all moral, social and economic arguments for the slave trade. When discussing the detrimental effects of the trade on Africans, he asked, 'Does the King of Barbissin want brandy? He has only to send his troops, in the night time, to burn and desolate a village; the captives will serve as commodities that may be bartered with the British trader.'

Wilberforce always refused to ridicule his opponents or present them as ogres, but instead he portrayed them as misguided in their belief that the slave trade made moral or financial sense. His marathon speech in May 1789 culminated with the words, 'Let not parliament be the only body that is not insensible to the principles of national justice. Let us make reparation to Africa, so far as we can, by establishing a trade upon true commercial principles, and we shall soon find the rectitude of our conduct rewarded by the benefits of a regular and growing commerce.'

Wilberforce's parliamentary colleague Edmund Burke, himself no slouch as an orator, likened his speech to 'the remains of Grecian eloquence'. Wilberforce's stellar performance was followed by worthy contributions from Prime Minister Pitt and Charles James Fox, a leading Whig MP.

Most abolitionist politicians like Wilberforce and Fox believed firmly that the slave trade was immoral and unjust, and their parliamentary speeches were thus infused with a passion born of conviction. The same could not be said for their opponents, and it was hard for even the most adept political orator to fire up colleagues on the sanctity of the slave trade. The slave-supporting MPs' approach was to appeal to the purse strings rather than the heartstrings and to point to the huge revenues accrued from the slave trade. It seems that in 1789, parliamentarians were more focused on the treasury coffers than African coffles.

The parliamentary debate was adjourned due to indecision in the House and when it resumed over a week later, apologist MPs regained their poise and the vote was defeated by 163 to 88. Although the abolitionists had been beaten on this occasion, they had not lost the war and Wilberforce and his colleagues looked upon this defeat as a sign of real progress.

8

Calling Time on the Slave Trade

Although parliament appeared full of slave trade supporting MPs, not for the first time the politicians in the House would soon be out of touch with public opinion. The Quakers' excellence for organization saw the mass distribution of anti-slavery reports, pamphlets and essays throughout the country. Similarly, because Britain was far from a literate society at that time, public talks and meetings were organized in towns and cities to hammer home the abolitionist message. Committees were also established up and down the country and what began as a meeting of 12 men soon developed into a national movement involving thousands of men and women.

Additionally, the anti-slavery movement included Africans such as Olaudah Equiano, who in 1789 published his autobiography before embarking on a national tour in order to promote both his work and the anti-slavery cause. Equiano's travels would take him to the four corners of the British Isles and make him the most well-known African of his time, speaking out passionately against the evils of the slave trade and slavery. His friend Quobna Ottobah Cugoano also joined Equiano in the growing abolitionist movement.

Cugoano was born in what is now Ghana in the 1750s. Like many of his peers, he was enslaved and taken to the West Indian island of Grenada. His master brought him to Britain during which time he obtained his freedom. Like Equiano, he was a man of faith and was baptized in 1773 as a sign of both his newly discovered freedom and his belief in Jesus Christ. Unlike Equiano, however, he chose to call himself 'John Stuart' – the name he took after his baptism. In the year in which the Committee for the Abolition of the African Slave Trade was formed, Cugoano published his own discourse on slavery – *Thoughts and Sentiments on the Evil and Wicked Traffic of the Slavery and Commerce of the Human Species*. In contrast to many of his white counterparts, Cugoano called for the immediate emancipation of all Africans, as well as the ending of the slave trade. Another noted African freedom fighter was Ignatius Sancho, who was born on a slave ship and whose letters and writings against slavery made him a noted figure in the abolition movement. He was also reported to be the first known African Britain to vote in a British election and gained fame in his time as the 'extraordinary negro'.

It should come as no surprise that Africans were involved in the campaign to end the slave trade as it was clearly in their best interests. In many parts of Africa, the West Indies and even Britain, no African – regardless of his status – was entirely free from the clutches of slave traders, who were on the lookout for Africans to work on West Indian plantations. One of the reasons why Equiano was keen to leave the Americas when he obtained his freedom was the fear that some unscrupulous slave trader may have forced him back into slavery. As Simon Schama points out, Equiano's 'manumission was no warranty against enslavement [and in] the years that followed he was often threatened with re-enslavement'.[1]

In such a rapacious society, a black skin equalled slavery money and no African was safe. It was therefore in the best interests of the educated, liberated Africans to fight for their enslaved brothers and sisters lest it became a 'today for you, tomorrow for me' scenario. The work of these African freedom fighters was also important because it dispelled many of the misconceptions that white people held about Africans at the time. In some British people's minds, Africans were either 'savages', 'pagans' or similar to 'children without opinions', and yet here were Equiano and his friends, helping to totally debunk these theories through powerful, articulate speeches and witty, forceful letters.

The British public turned out in good numbers to hear Equiano speak. His book-tour and speeches took him to Scotland and Northern Ireland and he was able with Clarkson and the other abolitionists to make the British public aware of the cruelty of the slave trade. Their combined efforts resulted in the boycott of slave-produced West Indian sugar. Most people today associate boycotts with a refusal to purchase items from questionable foreign regimes or dubious corporate business practices, but in the 1790s the sugar boycott was against sugar grown in the British West Indies. The boycott was arguably the first mass refusal by British people to purchase a product and it captured the imagination of rich and poor alike, who chose to drink their hot beverages without the sweetening aid.

Clarkson pointed out, 'There was no town, through which I passed, in which there was not someone... who has left off the sugar... By the best computation I was able to make... no fewer than three hundred thousand persons had abandoned the use of sugar.'[2] Unfortunately, many forgot that the same substance also went into the cakes, biscuits and jam that accompanied their tea and coffee and so the great British public continued to eat these sugar-laden items. But in spite of this, the abolitionists showed that consumer power had the potential to make both the government and the mighty sugar lobby sit up and take notice.

The *pièce de résistance* of the abolition campaign was Josiah Wedgwood's anti-slavery seal of a kneeling, chained African uttering the words, 'Am I not a man and a brother?'* Wedgwood was a Quaker and a joint-founder of the Committee for the Abolition of the African Slave Trade, and he allowed this iconic image to be reproduced on a range of paraphernalia.

In reference to Wedgwood's cameos, Thomas Clarkson wrote, 'Mr Wedgwood made a liberal donation… among his friends. I received no less than five hundred. They, to whom they were sent… gave them away, likewise. They were soon in different parts of the kingdom.'³ Clarkson observed that 'women of substance wore brooches emblazoned with image', much as wristbands and badges are worn to show solidarity with a campaign or good cause today. Items such as snuffboxes, purses and crockery carried the cameo image to remind the public of the horrors of the slave trade. A similar cameo was subsequently produced in 1826 to emphasize the suffering of African women during slavery with the words, 'Am I not a woman and a sister?'

One of the amazing aspects of the movement was the way that it cut across boundaries of class, gender and ethnicity and produced a hitherto unknown form of solidarity. The urban poor labouring in factories, for example, could identify with the exploitation of Africans. The eighteenth century was one of rapid transformation in which country gave way to town, and agricultural was matched by industrial. A series of inventions during the century enabled the industrialization of spinning and weaving and heralded the rise of factories and industrialized towns.

---

* Many African heritage groups find this image very problematic because of the subservient, pleading posture of the chained African. It has been argued that the image helped to create the belief that Africans were waiting for Englishmen to free them from enslavement.

Workers in these new factories often faced 80-hour weeks and children frequently formed the backbone of this new labour force. Death and maiming were common occurrences – the factory reforms and the movement for greater workers' rights would only occur in the nineteenth century.

In Britain, the late eighteenth century was characterized by the birth of the Industrial Revolution and the rise of work-related exploitation. Although British workers were not slaves, they were brutalized by factory owners in their attempt to increase both production and profits. Moreover, as Eric Hobsbawm pointed out in his seminal book *Industry and Empire*,[4] enslaved Africans and Lancashire workers were inextricably linked by cotton; Africans grew the cotton in North America and it was then transported to Britain where textile workers turned the material into products which were subsequently exported to Africa and the Americas.

White women could also relate to the powerlessness felt by the Africans in servitude, especially African women. According to the academic Vron Ware, 'women were ready to link their own subordination with that of black people by referring to the Christian ideal of inner strength that might be possessed by the physically and mentally weak…'.[5] In fact, one of the first novels to be written by a woman, the poet Aphra Behn's *Oroonoko or the Royal Slave*, which was published in 1688, dealt with the subject of slavery. The novel dealt with a handsome African prince, Oroonoko, who is captured, enslaved and taken to Suriname in South America. While there, he leads a rebellion which is brutally put down by local whites. Oroonoko is defiant to the last, even smoking his pipe while being chopped to death. The book was a bestseller for its time and helped to change certain perceptions about Africans, especially African men, by downplaying the traditional emphasis on the 'savage' and highlighting the fact that

Africans could be romantic and knew all about 'love and loss'.

Female involvement in the anti-slavery movement began at the outset of abolitionist activity, and Quaker women such as Mary Arthington and Catherine Elam of Leeds, Anne Hirst of Sheffield, Mary Hanbury of Stoke Newington, London, Susanna Boone of Birmingham and Catherine Fox of Falmouth were subscribers to the main Abolition Society to end the slave trade.

In reality, women played diverse roles in this prolonged campaign with some carrying out 'behind the scenes' manoeuvring – persuading a husband or father to support the campaign either politically or financially. Some were involved in direct participation while other women, such as the wives or daughters of the evangelical abolitionists – especially those in the Clapham Sect – were considered the 'guardians of religion and morality, an attitude which encouraged men to take heed of women's views on a topic such as slavery'.[6]

Women also played a more direct role as the prime movers in the emergence of abolition societies and contributed heavily to the upkeep of the existing organizations. Again, it was Quaker women who took the lead. In 1787, the same year as the official Quaker-led Committee for the Abolition of the African Slave Trade was formed, the *Manchester Mercury* newspaper published a letter from an anonymous woman encouraging the ladies of Manchester to sign petitions and give money 'for some parliamentary interference in favour of the oppressed Africans'.[7]

It must be noted that during the late eighteenth century, women were denied the vote, had little access to education and were under the legal authority of their husbands. The writer and feminist campaigner Mary Wollstonecraft used her seminal *A Vindication of the Rights of Women* to compare the position of women in British society with that of the enslaved African. In Wollstonecraft's opinion, educational boundaries kept women in a position of ignorance and slavish dependence. She also wrote that society encouraged women, like the African, to be docile, but although women 'may be convenient slaves... slavery will have its constant effect, degrading the master and the abject dependent'.[8]

Interestingly, Wollstonecraft's main detractor was the abolitionist Hannah More who took exception to Wollstonecraft's support for the French Revolution and the removal of corrupt monarchs, and her general championing of women's rights. Hannah More, who was a member of the Clapham Sect, has been described by one writer as 'pushy, humourless and complacent and could be unctuously sycophantic where influential men were concerned, whether they were politician, peers, ecclesiastics or cultural lions such as Samuel Johnson and David Garrick'.[9] Although this criticism does appear harsh, it reflects the divided opinions of More's legacy and the apparent contradictions in her life and attitudes. More was without doubt one of the leading female abolitionists of her time, although she is probably better remembered for her educational work among Britain's poor and the reformation of manners among the upper classes during the reign of George III.

Hannah More was born on 2 February 1745, the same year as Olaudah Equiano, on the outskirts of Bristol. By all accounts she was a good student who excelled in her studies and it was said that she spoke Latin, Greek, Spanish and French. After her studies, she embarked on a teaching career and with the assistance of her elder sister, Mary, opened a school for young ladies in Bristol in 1758. The school prospered both numerically and financially and enabled the More family to move to a more sought-after house in Bristol in the early 1760s.

Bristol's involvement in the slave trade had transformed the small town into a thriving city with an artistic life and social scene to equal that of any British city at that time. More developed her interest in poetry and playwriting and joined the city's literary circles, and by the mid 1760s she was part of the Theatre Royal, Bristol, and considered the leading actors of the day her close friends. Unfortunately, her romantic liaisons were never as successful as those of the characters in her literary works. She was forced to call off her prolonged engagement to Edward Turner when it became obvious to her, and to everyone else, that Turner had no intention of making her Mrs Turner. More managed to obtain what is now called 'palimony' from Turner and the £200 a year she received from her former lover enabled her to abandon teaching and move to London.

More swapped Bristol's bright lights for London's, and became part of the capital's literary and social life, joining the Blue Stocking Circle and making friends with one of Britain's leading actors of the day, David Garrick. Her circle of friends also included Sir Joshua Reynolds and, after an initial misunderstanding, the renowned Dr Samuel Johnson. More's friendship with Garrick in particular grew and, under his guidance, her tragedy *Percy* was staged at Covent Garden in 1777.

But More was never fortunate in close relationships and she interpreted the tragic death of Garrick in 1779 as a sign that she should abandon the 'frivolity' of her current existence for a more pious lifestyle. Consequently, she discarded the writer's quill and embraced evangelical Christianity. Equally, clergymen such as Dr Beilby Porteus, who later became the Bishop of London, and Revd John Newton replaced actors as her friends and confidants. Both Porteus and Newton were known abolitionists and More's friendship with them

183

definitely kindled her interest in the anti-slave trade movement. In 1788 she wrote the poem 'Slavery', which included the words:

'While the chill North with thy bright ray is blest,
Why should fell darkness half the South invest?
Was it decreed, fair Freedom! at thy birth,
That thou shou'd'st ne'er irradiate all the earth?
While Britain basks in thy full blaze of light.'[10]

More also formed a friendship with William Wilberforce and became the living embodiment of his task to 'reform manners'. If Wesley and the Methodists appeared to concentrate their work on the poor, Hannah More focused on the wealthy farmers and landowners, many of whom were known for their penchant for carousing. With the help of local clergy, she encouraged them to curb their excessive drinking and coarse behaviour in favour of a more sedate, spiritual existence. William Cobbett, no friend of the evangelical movement to end slavery, would describe her as the 'Bishop in Petticoats'.

Other detractors considered Hannah More to be an agent of the wealthy who championed deference and piety. A good example of this was the *Cheap Repository Tracts*, a series of well-written, moralistic pamphlets which began in 1795 and displayed her fondness for the poor, the monarchy and the status quo. Partly subsidized by the Clapham Sect in order to be sold cheaply, they would go on to sell over 2 million copies within a year of publication.

More was also fond of moving in royal circles and was often seen in the company of the children of King George III. She was a staunch royalist who had little time for anyone who criticized the monarchy, and she would combine her love for the royal family with her zeal for moral issues to write material on the two themes, the main publication being *Hints Towards Forming the Character of a Young Princess*, written in 1805 for the young Princess Charlotte.

With the advance of years, More gradually withdrew from society. However, age did not wither her support for the anti-slavery movement or diminish her commitment to promoting the gospel (she was a supporter of the British and Foreign Bible Society). She continued to give money to help the cause of the poor and spoke about the need to improve moral values with anyone who would listen. More also provided guidance for a younger generation of luminaries such as the historian, poet and politician Thomas Babington Macaulay, the poet Samuel Taylor Coleridge and the prison reformer Elizabeth Fry. Hannah More died in September 1833 – the same year that slavery was abolished in the British colonies and a few months after Wilberforce's own death.

The last word on Hannah More should be left to the historian Linda Colley, who is more a detractor than a devotee, but who suggests, 'at her death... [More] was worth £30,000. Self-made and a life-long spinster, More had become the first British woman ever to make a fortune with her pen, and this fact alone should warn us against seeing her simply as a conservative figure'.[11]

It would be wrong, however, to suggest that all female abolitionists were well-heeled, educated women with time on their hands, as working class women from all parts of Britain participated in the anti-slavery movement in the eighteenth and nineteenth centuries. The anti-slave trade movement was one that even some British factory owners supported, at least in the early days, because abolition initially seemed to pose no direct threat to their interests. In fact, many welcomed their workers focusing on the rights of those overseas rather than on their own rights. Having said that, many of the working class activists used the skills they had acquired from the anti-slavery movement to fight for the rights of British factory workers. This was particularly the case for the campaigners who had been fired up by reading Thomas Paine's book *The Rights of Man* and used the slavery issue as a practice run for the working class battles that were to come. One can argue that it was fashionable or politically correct to support abolition during the late 1780s, although all this was soon to change.

Events on the other side of the channel had always cast a long shadow over British affairs. The French were not only rivals in war but also in commerce. By the 1780s, they had possession of the smaller section of the island of Hispaniola, St Domingue, which was at the time the most productive and financially lucrative sugar-based economy in the world. The Prime Minister, William Pitt, was always concerned that Britain should not end its participation in slave trading without a similar agreement from France and was especially worried that Britain's removal from the slave trade would leave the door open for its French rivals to monopolize the slave trade. However, in 1789 France was overtaken by a revolution preaching liberty, equality and fraternity. The French Revolution was initially welcomed by some of the abolitionists. Thomas Clarkson believed that the initial French calls for liberty would result in the country turning its back on the slave trade and, full of revolutionary ire, he made his way to Paris on a fact-finding tour. There he met with the French writer and thinker Jacques Pierre Brissot, who had founded 'The Society of the Friends of the Blacks' or *Société des amis des Noirs* or *Amis des Noirs*, and advised him on campaign strategy.

The French Revolution, however, would lose its appeal for many in Britain and a few years after the initial heady days of revolt, the high-minded revolutionary principles dissipated into a frenzy of violence and revenge. This resulted in an obvious loss of support from the wealthy in British society and the Revolution helped to split the well-formed alliances as well as the abolitionist movement itself. The conservative abolitionists were particularly alarmed by events in France and feared that it would stoke up similar sentiments in Britain. Believing in a divine order of society, and not wanting to lose their own heads, conservative abolitionists denounced the Revolution as seditious and looked to curtail the wrath of their more revolutionary colleagues.

The real blow to the more radical abolitionists came with the revolution in St Domingue, which was a disaster waiting to happen. A careful analysis of most slave societies will reveal that all were subject to both passive and active resistance, and outright uprisings – although not common – did occur in these societies. The St Domingue rebellion was notable, however, because it was fuelled by ideas emanating from revolutionary France, which provided a political framework for an activity that was usually characterized by wanton violence. This particular revolution was also noted for its barbarity: during the uprising, the Africans mercilessly slaughtered whites in their struggle to free themselves from an equally brutal system.

Public opinion in Britain was firmly behind the unfortunate white elite in St Domingue and the London-based Society of West Indian Planters and Merchants wasted no time in using the violence and destruction of the Revolution as confirmation of the maligned influence of the abolitionists. They called on all 'right-minded' abolitionists (those with conservative tendencies and overseas properties) to identify with the losses suffered by the French property-owning classes in St Domingue, which obviously included sugar planters.

Most British abolitionists wanted to free the Africans with conditions attached so that after the slavery system was dismantled, real power would still remain in the hands of the colonial (white) masters. It was the case that most abolitionists, despite their relative progressiveness, were still either unconditioned or reluctant to perceive Africans as the agents of their own freedom. Radical historians have even argued that some abolitionists had been seduced by the Wedgwood anti-slavery cameo, which presented a comfortable or safe image of the supplicant African looking heavenwards to God or the white man to free him from his enslavement.

The French Revolution was, ultimately, no friend of the anti-slavery movement. It polarized opinion in Britain, making foes of potential allies. The Church of England, always a lukewarm supporter of abolition, reflected the views of its constituents and clergy, when it encouraged 'all good Christians to distance themselves from the St Domingue uprisings'. Many clergymen, including bishops, had investments in West Indian slavery: the Society for the Propagation of the Gospel owned plantations in Barbados and therefore had no wish to see similar events take place on that island to the ruin of their financial interests.

Similarly, the writings of Revd Raymond Harris, a clergyman with the knack of twisting the most innocuous of Bible verses to justify slavery, came into their own during this period. Harris' infamous publication *Scriptural Researches on the Licitness of the Slave Trade Showing its Conformity with the Principles of the Natural and Revealed Religion in the Sacred Writings of the Word of God*, was not only a rebuke for those trying to use the Bible to condemn the slave trade, but also a considered response on the idea that there was little contradiction between the scriptures and enslavement. Harris' book was dedicated to Liverpool's mayor as well as aldermen, bailiffs and councilmen, all of whom had direct links to the slave trade, giving rise to the rumour that Harris had been paid by slave-trading interests to write the book. Despite the long-winded title, Harris' work was extremely well received and sold well in the late 1780s and onwards.

Not all church folk shared Harris' ideas. The great evangelical founder of Methodism, John Wesley, had denounced slavery in no uncertain terms in his 1774 treatise *Thoughts on Slavery* and had encouraged Wilberforce in his work. Wilberforce needed this support as the abolitionists had found themselves on the back foot due to the St Domingue Revolution. Slave trade supporting parliamentarians, such as the Liverpudlian former war hero Banastre Tarleton, argued that the work of the abolitionists would result in similar revolutions to that witnessed in St Domingue. As we have seen, the abolitionists lost the vote and their defeat received a literally ringing endorsement from the churches in Bristol, whose bells rejoiced in celebration.

Chief among the Christian abolitionists were the 'Clapham Sect', a group of wealthy Church of England evangelicals who lived in the leafy village of Clapham, South London in the late eighteenth century. The Clapham Sect took an interest in a range of social reform activities, including the ending of the slave trade. Wilberforce was part of the group, and the Sect was the living embodiment of his 'twin objects' – the ending of the slave trade and the reformation of manners (moral values).

Other prime movers in the group included Granville Sharp, Zachary Macaulay, who went on to be governor of Sierra Leone, James Stephen, who was a lawyer and Henry Thornton, who was MP for Southwark. All members were as much concerned with the Africans' spiritual well-being as they were with ending the slave trade. From their 'spiritual' base at Holy Trinity Church on Clapham Common, they planned and strategized how to improve society's apparent moral and social failings – as typified by William Hogarth's paintings of the era.

The 'Saints' – as the Caribbean historian, Eric Williams, pejoratively described them – were connected by faith, friendship, business and marriage. William Wilberforce was the second cousin of Henry Thornton, who was the son of a former director of the Bank of England. Thomas Babington, MP for Leicestershire, was married to Zachary Macaulay's sister, while James Stephen married Wilberforce's sister. Moreover, most lived within a stone's throw of each other near to Clapham Common, although not everyone linked to the Clapham Sect did. Hannah More lived in Bristol, Thomas Babington in Leicestershire, and Granville Sharpe only moved to Clapham when he was very advanced in years.

Much has been written about the Victorians, their values and the work they carried out among the poor. In truth, it was Georgian Christians such as the Clapham Sect who were the standard bearers of a new type of social and moral agitation. It is possible today to see the legacy of the Clapham Sect's work in the Sunday School movement. These establishments were indicative of their activities among the urban poor; lashings of scripture accompanied by healthy doses of lectures on good behaviour. When not focusing on the earthly and spiritual well-being of Britons, the Sect acted as the forerunner for the more strategic British missionary work that was to take place in Africa and Asia during the nineteenth century. Members of the Clapham Sect helped to establish the Bible Society, Church Mission Society and a whole host of philanthropic groups.

Such well-to-do philanthropy is often denounced as patronizing today and there is little doubt that the Sect's work among the poor did flirt with condescension. They believed in concepts such as the 'deserving and undeserving poor' and a 'place for everyone and everyone knowing his place'. Although carried out with the sincerest of intentions, the Sect's work with the poor mirrored its activities with Africans, who were seen as wretched creatures in need of assistance from their betters. And their work was always to remove these 'unfortunate beings' from drudgery, but never to put them on an equal footing.

But having said that, alongside the Quakers they were one of the first groups to recognize the core humanity of African people and they were tireless fighters for the rights of Africans in Britain, the West Indies and the continent of Africa itself. Their approach to solving the 'problems' of African people would perhaps be frowned upon today, but it was considered very radical in its time. The Clapham Sect played a pivotal role in ending the slave trade and making a vast swathe of British society aware of the human rights of Africans.

The Clapham Sect would have looked on in horror as they saw the situation in France quickly deteriorate. Many within the group had been in favour of the Revolution initially, but they probably shuddered at its departure from the heady ideals of 1789 to the tyranny and violence of the mid 1790s. The situation in France openly questioned the priorities and principles of all within Britain. Prime Minister Pitt argued that he had to overlook the slavery question due to the pressing issue of protecting his country from a workers-led revolution and French designs on Britain. Additionally, with one eye on the finances, he weighed up the possibilities of a British invasion of the slave-free state of St Domingue in order to reinstate European colonial rule on that section of the island. Pitt knew that St Domingue had been France's most lucrative West Indian colony and he wanted it to become a similar money-spinner for Britain. In 1794, the financial arguments won out and Britain embarked on an ill-fated attempt to capture St Domingue. It was soon to experience a similar fate to the French forces.

Wilberforce found himself faced with a choice between two equally unsatisfactory options and appeared compromised by events beyond his control. He refused to condemn the British invasion of St Domingue, which if successful would reinstate slavery, and domestically he sided with laws that suppressed seditious activity. Although he considered himself an independent with regard to his parliamentary voting record, Wilberforce was a conservative at heart and as such he was deeply opposed to any activity threatening king or country. Consequently, he supported Pitt's Gagging Acts, which banned meetings of over 50 people, and instructed local magistrates to arrest anyone suspected of spreading seditious libel. He also sided with the Combination Acts that prevented the formation of trade unions among the workers, leading to a tirade against him by the social activist William Cobbett.

In Cobbett's opinion, Wilberforce was more interested in the 'Negroes' of the West Indies than the British white working class labourers and, using language that would be described as racist today, he suggested, 'you, Wilberforce, are petitioning for the blacks, I am resolved to see if I cannot find somebody to join with me in a petition for the Whites. You seem to have great affection for the fat and lazy and laughing and singing and dancing Negroes, they it is for whom you feel compassion: I feel for the care-worn, the ragged, the hard-pinched, the ill-treated, and the beaten down and trampled upon labouring classes of England, Scotland, and Ireland, to whom, as I said before, you do all the mischief that it is in your power to do...'.[12]

Both the political and public thrust of the anti-slave trade movement in Britain was undoubtedly stymied by fears that the French wanted to export its revolutionary ideas across the Channel. A further body blow to the movement occurred with the retirement of Thomas Clarkson in July 1794. Clarkson had what we would now consider a nervous breakdown, caused both by overwork and a sense of frustration at the abolition campaign's lack of significant progress in parliament. He was also bitterly disappointed with the direction the French Revolution had taken in the 1790s. Unlike the other abolitionists, Clarkson had backed the Revolution to the hilt and so as the situation went awry, he saw his reputation take a battering. He was forced to retire from the campaign for nearly a decade. Unable to work, he had to sell his shares in the Sierra Leone Company and rely on the benevolence of Wilberforce and other colleagues to keep the creditors away.

As the eighteenth century drew to a close, Wilberforce found himself alone in the campaign and even his great resolve began to wilt. His once rock-solid friendship with Prime Minister Pitt had suffered greatly due to the latter's preoccupation with France and some of his old allies in parliament had either died (Edmund Burke in 1797), resigned from office (Fox) or switched sides on the debate (Windham). Moreover, the great strain of shouldering the bulk of the work took its toll on Wilberforce. In truth, he never fully recovered from the illness that had almost taken his life in 1789, and during the last few years of the eighteenth century, his health continued to suffer. The irony was that when both the anti-slave trade movement and Wilberforce were at their lowest ebbs, motions in parliament to end the slave trade were defeated by only a handful of votes in 1796 and 1798 respectively. But despite these close calls, parliament appeared to turn its back on the abolition movement.

Wilberforce kept his own counsel on the subject during the first three years of the nineteenth century, and politically the situation was relatively free from contention for the pro-slave-trading alliance. Their main adversaries, the Committee for the Abolition of the African Slave Trade, met infrequently between 1797 and 1804, largely due to the passing of draconian laws to counteract any seditious activities that were linked to Napoleon.

Statistics linked to the slave trade also reveal that Liverpool continued to flourish as a slaving port. Moreover, bullish absentee West Indian planters (invariably men who owned plantations in the West Indies but left them in the care of estate managers in order to live lavish lifestyles back in Britain) were only too happy to regale concerned listeners with the horrors taking place in St Domingue and the need for stronger laws to curtail African ambitions elsewhere in the West Indies.

The writer of the Old Testament book of Ecclesiastes suggested that 'For everything there is a season, and a time for every matter under heaven.' After several moribund years in the early nineteenth century, events were about to turn in favour of the abolitionists. The first key event was the return to physical and mental health of Thomas Clarkson in 1804. Clarkson's enthusiasm had energized the initial countrywide campaign and his absence through illness was one of the main reasons for the campaign's temporary decline. Clarkson's reappearance proved to be the catalyst for the campaign to be reinvigorated and also coincided with the emergence of newer faces from the Clapham Sect such as Zachary Macaulay and James Stephen.

Macaulay had been the governor of Sierra Leone and was also one of the few abolitionists to have personally experienced the travails of the Middle Passage, having travelled back to Britain from Sierra Leone (via the West Indies) on board a slaver. This enabled him to provide an eyewitness account of the full horrors of the Middle Passage. James Stephen was an even more impressive figure and regarded as the real brains among the movement, his intellectual prowess as a lawyer proving to be invaluable to abolitionist MPs.

The abolitionists' cause was further helped by Admiral Lord Nelson's defeat of Napoleon at the Battle of Trafalgar in 1805. His rout of Napoleon in the maritime battle removed any possibility of a French sea invasion of Britain. However, Nelson had little time for the abolitionists, denouncing their influence as the 'damnable doctrine of Wilberforce and his hypocritical allies', and he was a constant foe in parliament.

The hopes of the abolitionists coincided with a changing mood in Britain – even among conservative parliamentarians. People began to believe that the slave trade was not in keeping with British pretensions as the world's leading moral and cultural force. Instead efforts to end the slave trade appeared in keeping with Britain's so-called historic role as the true bastion of freedom and champion of human rights. In the early nineteenth century, many in Britain believed that the ending of the slave trade was wholly compatible with other ambitions such as being the world's leading industrial nation.

The Industrial Revolution, which began in the late eighteenth century, spawned many technological developments that totally transformed living and working conditions for vast swathes of the population. These changes were accompanied by further scientific, cultural and political developments that placed Britain at the forefront of everything modern. This was in stark contrast to slavery that relied on slave labour as opposed to free labour, and thrived on monopolies rather than liberalized trade. The disparity between a British factory and a West Indian plantation was similar to a modern-day office in which some staff use computers, while others use manual typewriters. In short, the slave trade, indeed, slavery itself, appeared out of keeping with British ideas of progression and efficiency.

Equally, the slave trade issue enabled Britain to seize the moral high ground from its main rivals, France and the United States. Both countries boasted frequently about freedom, equality and fraternity, but their actions often contradicted their words. The United States had a constitution that proclaimed liberty and other lofty ideals, but considered Africans to be only three-fifths of a human being. By the early nineteenth century, it was still a slavery-based nation, importing enslaved Africans in such numbers that African arrivals outnumbered white immigration in some states in the United States. Moreover, several US presidents owned enslaved Africans and slavery-run cotton plantations. Similarly, French pretensions of liberty and equality resulted in the gallows for French royalty and the aristocracy, and a similar fate awaited any other enemy of the Revolution. Then there was the chaos of a Napoleon-backed venture to reinstate slavery to the newly liberated country of St Domingue.

While others were enslaving or oppressing Africans, Britain could boast that it was a haven for those fleeing oppression. Many interpreted Lord Mansfield's edict of 1772 as the end of slavery in the nation, believing that all enslaved Africans who arrived on its shores were now automatically free. This was clearly not the situation, but it suited some to believe that 'the air of England is too pure for a slave to breathe, and so everyone who breathes it becomes free'. Britain could highlight its honoured promise of liberty to the Africans who fought on its side during the American War of Independence. Although Britain lost the war, it did not abandon the Africans but instead encouraged them to go to Nova Scotia and then resettle in Sierra Leone.

The role of religion ought not to be excluded from this. The evangelical revival in the second half of the eighteenth century had a profound affect in Britain, awakening hearts and minds to all matters spiritual as well as material. It also gave credence to the belief that there was a divine mandate underpinning Britain's claim to be the world's moral compass. Evangelical Christianity highlighted the ethical inconsistencies of the slave trade, a view bolstered by influential sections of the Church of England which eventually found its voice and its confidence to speak out against the slave trade by the early nineteenth century.

Primary among the champions was Dr Bielby Porteus, who held bishoprics in Chester and London. Like Wilberforce, Porteus was an evangelical and his writings railed against the slave trade and gave some much-needed church backing to the abolition campaign. It was one thing to have individuals with loose church connections attacking the slave trade but quite another to have one of its most senior figures lambasting it as immoral and unethical. Crucially, as Bishop of London Porteus had jurisdiction over the Church of England's decision-making processes in the West Indies and during his time in office the number of missionaries sent to the region increased greatly.

Moreover, the abolitionists took advantage of the country's anti-French feelings to argue that the slave trade was against Britain's economic interests. They used statistics to show that far too many British slave ships transporting enslaved Africans to West Indian colonies were controlled by France and the United States. The abolitionists also used guile to drive a wedge between West Indian planters and British slave traders, attempting to convince the West Indian planters that the slave trade was a sinking ship which they ought to abandon before it was too late.

The planters for their part were aware that some abolitionists were against slave trading but not slavery itself and that alliances could be made with these individuals or groups if the planters were more humane to Africans. Wilberforce even reassured the planters that plantation slavery could not end because Africans were not in a position to look after themselves. As a result, some planters and estate managers embarked on the crude practice of encouraging 'breeding' among their enslaved Africans in order to wean themselves off imports if and when slave trading became illegal.

Moreover, MP James Stephen used his in-depth knowledge of maritime law and his familiarity with the slave trade to reinforce the point that slavery was against Britain's ultimate economic interests. With Wilberforce's assistance, he raised the issue in a parliament that had become increasingly receptive to the abolitionist message. The apologists countered with their usual suggestion that Britain's withdrawal would serve the financial interests of its rivals, namely France. However, this argument carried less weight after 1804 when St Domingue became an independent nation called Haiti, which was free from both slavery and French domination.

The slave-trading apologists came out fighting, mounting a desperate campaign to safeguard their threatened financial interests. They took out adverts in the press, urged their parliamentarians to use every opportunity to speak in favour of the trade and especially promoted the numerous economic benefits of slave trading. But the abolitionists countered with a propaganda campaign of their own which included thousands of petitions, showing that the great British public was now firmly against the slave trade.

The death of William Pitt in 1806 also worked in the abolitionists' favour. The ravages of battling Napoleon combined with an alleged fondness for alcohol had taken their toll on the health of Wilberforce's long-time friend and quenched his ardour to end the slave trade. At the time of his death, Pitt was more of a hindrance than a help to the abolition movement and many welcomed the arrival of his successor as prime minister, Lord Grenville, because of his influence within the House of Lords. The Lords during that era was a powerful beast, capable of destroying parliamentary bills that came before it.

Many of Wilberforce's previous parliamentary motions had fallen foul in the Lords thanks to men such as Banastre Tarleton, Lord Nelson and the Duke of Clarence, son of King George III. Allies were therefore necessary in the Upper House, and one who combined these duties with that of prime minister would be invaluable. A new prime minister was also the ideal stimulus for the abolition campaign and Lord Grenville wasted no time in overseeing the passing of the Importation Restriction Bill in 1806 which upheld many of Stephen's proposals.

The way was now open for the eventual ending of Britain's involvement in the slave trade. In desperation, the slave trade lobby mounted one last defence, pointing out that the trade was still a lucrative proposition and that ships leaving Liverpool made handsome profits of £15,000 a time. In the Lords, the Duke of Clarence, Lord Hawkesbury and others of a similar mindset were mobilized to end the madness. Unfortunately for them, the abolitionists had won the argument and the bill to end British involvement in the slave trade was passed by 283 votes to 16; King George III, often described as 'mad' by his critics, gave it Royal Assent on 25 March 1807.

9

Set All Free

Such is the lack of awareness throughout our society about chattel enslavement that many confuse the ending of the slave trade with the ending of chattel enslavement itself. The Abolition Act of 1807 did not spell the end of slavery and the Act did not help the 500,000 Africans enduring the terror and violence of plantation slavery. However, the Act was the first major intervention in ending Transatlantic Slavery, and like Napoleon's defeat at Trafalgar a few years earlier, it was an important battle in a great war. It was important also because by 1807 Britain was one of the world's leading slave-trading nations, and with one flourish of the royal fountain pen, British ships were legally barred from partaking in slave trading.

The Act may have criminalized all British involvement in the slave trade, but slave traders – with one eye on profits – were willing to flout the law to meet the massive demand for enslaved Africans in many parts of the Americas. Britain may have turned her back on the slave trade, but Portugal, France and other slave-trading nations were willing to fill the gap left by Britain's withdrawal and there is little doubt that some of Britain's former competitors would have been delighted at the thought of one of the world's largest slave traders removing itself from the trade.

There is evidence also to suggest that, far from reducing the number of Africans transported across the Atlantic, the Act may even have actually stimulated the smuggling industry and other underhand means of trafficking Africans. According to the Caribbean historians Parry and Sherlock, 'The total number of slaves taken from West Africa after the Abolition Act may in fact have been greater than the total of those taken before that date; it is certain that both Cuba and Brazil imported greater numbers after 1808 than they did during the earlier period.'[1] And figures produced by the Cuban historian Louis Pérez reveal that 'the number of slaves increased almost threefold, accounting in 1827 for more than 40 per cent of the total population'.[2]

British slave-trading ventures had previously serviced the British colonies with Africans not only within the West Indies, but also those of her political and economic rivals such as the United States, Portugal, Holland and Spain. But for those countries still dependent on African labour to sustain their slave-based economies, the bottom line was about obtaining labourers and few cared whether they arrived legally or illicitly, as long as they came in sufficient numbers.

Aware that many in Britain would be tempted to flout the law, the British government dispatched the Royal Navy to thwart any unlawful slave trading. From 1807 onwards, the navy patrolled the African coastline and the mid-Atlantic deploying 'gunboat' diplomacy to intercept any ship suspected of slave trading. Such vessels were boarded and searched for enslaved Africans. Any Africans found on board were seized and subsequently returned to Africa, usually Sierra Leone. Any British merchant or captain found in possession of Africans to be used for the purposes of slave trading received a heavy fine, and by the 1820s the law was stiffened to make such illegal activity punishable by death. And yet, such were the profits to be made from the slave trade, that an increasing number of ships used all manner of subterfuge to ply their trade.

In July 1809, Zachary Macaulay suspected that at least 36 ships had sailed from Liverpool on slaving journeys since the 1807 Abolition Act. A typical ruse involved ships leaving British ports with one name and arriving in France or West Africa with another name, nationality and captain in order to conduct their slave trading. British ships also preferred to sail under a United States flag of convenience because the after-effects of the War of Independence had made any Royal Navy interventions diplomatically tricky. Thomas Clarkson saw clear evidence of illicit slave trading when he visited Liverpool in 1809 and was disturbed when he observed merchants selling goods such as manacles and chains for export to slave-trading nations such as Brazil and Cuba.

Between 1807–1820, the British government spent a lot of time and money convincing its European rivals to similarly turn their collective backs on slave trading. Some, such as France, would eventually agree to end the trade almost a decade after Britain, although France refused to cooperate with the British Navy's attempts to verify that its ships were not smuggling Africans. Spain followed suit a few years later but both European powers were half-hearted about the issue and slave trading continued to be an open business in ports like Nantes, where the profits from the trade were said to have amounted to 90 million francs in 1815. Portugal had the matter taken out of its hands when its prize possession of Brazil declared its independence in 1822.

Inertia had set in following parliament's passing of the Abolition Bill in 1807. After the inevitable backslapping and self-congratulation, the abolitionists remained split on what further action they ought to take, especially as the long, hard-won war had accounted for many lives. Equiano, who had travelled thousands of miles promoting his autobiography and the need for abolition, died a decade before the abolitionists could celebrate victory. The original poacher turned gamekeeper, John Newton, died in December 1807 at the ripe old age of 82. Unlike Equiano, he lived to see the end of an industry that had helped to make him wealthy for a time, but which ultimately had caused him great misery. Newton's lasting legacy to the abolition movement was the spiritual and moral advice he advanced to his protégé William Wilberforce.

Wilberforce remained ambiguous on the subject of emancipation. When discussing what they should abolish next after the passing of the Abolition Act, Wilberforce and fellow 'Claphamites' looked to ban the national lottery rather than slavery. Certain scholars are often critical of Wilberforce's commitment to ending slavery in the West Indies and put his hesitancy down to his belief that enslaved Africans were not ready for freedom and his fear of the wealthy, influential West Indian planters.

Equally Wilberforce, like many of his day, held the belief that God had created a world of defined roles. Some people were rulers – men of Wilberforce's ilk – while others were there to be ruled, such as the Africans. For Wilberforce, Africans had to be converted to Christianity and then subjected to the treatment reserved for children at that time – a mixture of compassion and chastisement. In 1807 he established The African Institution with colleagues in order to promote civilization and improvement on the African continent. The organization also sought to encourage other nations to end their human trafficking and trade in legitimate African resources.

Wilberforce was also often accused of naivety with regard to his belief that the ending of the slave trade would result in the eventual demise of chattel enslavement. This notion proposed that once starved of a ready source of workers, slavery would die a painful, albeit speedy, death. But what Wilberforce and others of a similar mindset underestimated was the level of smuggling and illicit slave trading that occurred after Britain's ban. They also overlooked the planters' crude attempts to 'breed' enslaved Africans in the Americas to help sustain the slave system, and the sheer stubbornness of British West Indian assemblies (systems of local government) which believed that slavery was fundamental to the continuing prosperity of their territories, a belief that would help ensure their continued fight to maintain the current system.

The more radical abolitionists such as Thomas Clarkson considered their slavery efforts to be unfinished business and urged the movement to continue working to end slavery. But before he wrote letters to parliamentarians urging them to do the same, Clarkson turned his attention to writing up his account of the African slave trade and its abolition. Although he was obviously a stalwart within the campaign, Clarkson's version of events suggested that he should take the main share of the credit for the Act being passed. However, his account failed to fully explain the decade of activity between the early 1790s and the turn of the century when he had temporarily retired from the movement. He also played down the full extent of Wilberforce's financial assistance when he was forced to withdraw from the campaign due to ill health. In truth, Clarkson's book was penned by a man basking in the adulation of having a sonnet written about him – 'To Thomas Clarkson' – by the esteemed poet William Wordsworth. They had become friends while Clarkson was recuperating from his nervous breakdown in the Lake District during the 1790s. For a time also, Clarkson was one of the most famous men in the country and appeared to relish his fame.

The abolitionists, however, faced an uphill task trying to encourage the British public of the need to end slavery. West

Indian slavery was clearly dehumanizing and based on fear and terror, but in terms of sheer work its brutal conditions were not so far removed from those of a British factory or a mine at that time. British factory owners had warned parliamentarians of the potential danger that reform on one side of the Atlantic might lead to similar reform being proposed within Britain. To some extent they were right, because during the period 1807–1820, sporadic social unrest and radical class-based activity increased significantly.

Men such as William Cobbett, Thomas Spence, Henry 'Orator' Hunt, Major John Cartwright and Sir Francis Burdett spread fear throughout both the heart of government and the ruling classes alike with their talk of workers' rights and greater political reform and representation. Moreover, the passing of the Corn Laws in 1815, coupled with a poor harvest the following year, caused bread prices to rise sharply and British workers soon began insisting on increased wages to help meet the rising cost of food. Their demands led to food riots across Britain.

The Peterloo Massacre in Manchester in 1819 involved over a thousand soldiers brutally bludgeoning a large crowd (including women and children) that had assembled to hear speakers brought together by the Manchester Patriotic Union Society, a political group that was agitating for both repeal of the Corn Laws and radical parliamentary reform. Eleven were killed and many more were injured and the incident was regarded as a heavy-handed response by the authorities to stifle public debate. These important domestic matters had distracted most of the abolition-supporting MPs, and if they were not voting in favour of policies that curtailed the influence of agitators and banned such public gatherings, they were nevertheless fixated by the Duke of Wellington's attempts to finish off Napoleon once and for all at Waterloo.

But if the abolitionists were unsure what action they should take to end slavery, enslaved Africans suffered no such doubts. They used every available opportunity to fight for their freedom and even subtle or small attempts to undermine plantation slavery formed part of this wider plan. Moreover, enslavement did not deter them from keeping abreast of both local and foreign news. Africans in both Africa and the West Indies were aware of Wilberforce and the work being done in Britain to end slavery, largely through careless dinner-table talk by West Indian planters. Those working as house slaves relayed this information to others on the plantation and, like a game of 'Chinese whispers', any parliamentary discussions on slavery were interpreted as 'free paper come' (immediate emancipation). This was not a case of African wishful thinking; rather they drew the logical conclusion that any discussions about their status as enslaved Africans would ultimately end in their freedom.

There is no evidence that Africans concurred with the opinion of certain abolitionists – and practically every West Indian planter – that they were 'not ready' for freedom. They undoubtedly wanted this and were willing to use any necessary means to obtain it. Moreover, the Haitian Revolution had shown them that there was no such thing as white dominance within plantation societies.

West Indian planters, however, adopted a very cavalier attitude towards some of the debates taking place in London about slavery. As far as they were concerned, any act of parliament that gave extra liberties to Africans and curtailed their own rights was to be ignored. This included parliamentary legislation ordering the registration of all enslaved Africans within the West Indies to curtail smuggling, and the need to improve the living and working conditions of Africans. The problem facing the planters was that Africans chose to pay attention to news coming from London and knew that both the planters and local assemblies were deliberately holding back on essential reforms. But in truth, some planters cared little about what their enslaved Africans thought and, like William Cobbett, believed the Africans to be dull, easily excitable and predisposed to laziness. Equally, any potential disquiet on a plantation could be overcome if the Africans were given the opportunity to sing and dance after a hard day's work. On the other hand, certain planters believed their Africans were artful and totally untrustworthy and watched their every move like an old-time CCTV system. West Indian planters also believed that Africans from particular ethnic groupings were more docile than others, or had more of a propensity to work hard. For instance, Jamaican planters regarded the Ashanti people (modern-day Ghana) as unruly with a natural disposition to rebel, while the 'Congoes in St Domingue were regarded by the planters... as the most tractable or "docile" of Africans'.[3] It is hard not to dismiss such ideas as nonsensical but many West Indian planters believed them. As such, Africans from certain ethnic groupings would fetch a higher price at slave markets because they were deemed better suited to slavery.

The men (and they were invariably men) who formed the Assemblies that ran the West Indian colonies were closely connected to the planters – some had family connections with planters or were even involved in the business themselves. They could not believe that Britain wanted to kill off such a lucrative moneymaking operation and many held the view that parliamentarians were out of touch with life in the West Indies. In an era in which there was no such thing as a fact-finding tour for MPs, many politicians were forced to rely on the opinions of whoever could shout the loudest or had the deepest pockets, to win their influence.

However, MPs were forced to sit up and take notice when West Indian matters began to have a direct impact on British interests. Such was the situation during the Bussa Revolt in Barbados in 1816. On this tiny West Indian island, the heightened talk of freedom, coupled with planter stubbornness to implement reforms, led to a marked increase in passive and active resistance from Africans. The Bussa Revolt, named after the enslaved African who led the rebellion, was the culmination of the many frustrations of the Africans and it became one of the greatest slave-led uprisings in history.

The revolt took place around Easter time and saw enslaved Africans interpreting the registration of slaves' reform as a sign of their forthcoming emancipation. When nothing occurred, some argued that they had been freed on Easter Monday, and that it was up to them to take their liberty by any means necessary. When the British finally managed to put down the rebellion, vast amounts of property had been destroyed and a great number of Africans had lost their lives. As with all failed acts of resistance, the gallows awaited the perpetrators.

Back in Britain, apathy typified the mood among the abolitionists between 1815–23. Some, like Wilberforce, still held on to the belief that the 1807 Abolition Act would help bring an end to slavery. Others, who considered this approach folly, called on their brothers and sisters to once again take up the cause of immediate freedom for all Africans. Thomas Clarkson, ever the activist, called on his erstwhile abolitionist colleagues and anyone else with an interest in ending slavery to join him for the 'final push'.

By 1823, a significant number of abolitionists had come around to Clarkson's way of thinking and began calling for a resurgence of the original movement in order to finally end slavery. The result of this effort was the founding of the Society for the Mitigation and Gradual Abolition of Slavery. Following close on its heels was the *Anti-Slavery Monthly Reporter*, the journal which became the mouthpiece for all anti-slavery activity.

And yet, for all its abhorrence of plantation slavery, the new organization still followed the path of 'abolition by stealth', which meant relative improvements in the conditions on plantations, and the treatment of Africans. Chief among their amelioration aims were an acknowledgment of slave marriages, a further day off work during the week so that Africans could attend churches on Sunday, and the granting of freedom to the offspring of enslaved Africans. In reality, the rather traditional agenda of the London Society for the Mitigation and Gradual Abolition of Slavery revealed that some within the organization had begun to believe the West Indian planters' propaganda which claimed that they were like fathers to their childlike Africans, who would not be able to cope if they were emancipated. Old hands such as Clarkson had very little time for this nonsensical planter misinformation and urged the group to be more radical in its aims. He was joined by newer recruits, mainly Quakers, who would subsequently accompany him on his travels to whip up support for the immediate ending of slavery.

Wilberforce, now an old man suffering from various illnesses, eventually realized that slavery would never end by its own volition and published *An Appeal to the Religion, Justice and Humanity of the Inhabitants of the British Empire on behalf of the Negro Slaves in the West Indies* in March 1823. Due to his failing health, Wilberforce allowed his fellow parliamentarian, Thomas Fowell Buxton, to submit a motion for amelioration on 15 May 1823. The motion included such concessions as 'the testimony of Africans be counted as admissible in court', the children of enslaved Africans 'be freed and educated', the use of the whip 'be limited, especially on women', and Africans 'receive formal religious instruction'. Most importantly, the parliamentary intervention pressed the case for gradual emancipation.

Lord Canning, leader of the House of Commons, immediately took exception to what he considered 'the rather radical nature' of the Bill and encouraged amendments, particularly the portion relating to 'gradual emancipation'. Canning's subsequent modifications encouraged parliament to improve the lot of enslaved Africans on plantations but sidestepped the issue of gradual freedom. He also suggested that it should be left to the colonial legislatures to implement these proposals, ensuring that the West Indian Assemblies had the right to ignore the legislation if they so wished. Like many in the House, Canning wanted to safeguard the financial interests of West Indian planters and had no desire to see them bankrupted through parliamentary changes.

Yet it was an indication of the stiff-necked attitude of the West Indian Assemblies that they chose to dismiss many of these toothless reforms without any real consideration. Both West Indian planters and governors feared that meddling would hinder the productiveness of their plantation societies and create unrest among Africans. They took particular exception to the limits placed on the use of the whip as in their minds slavery could not function without coercion, and the favoured tool to carry this out was the whip. It would not be an exaggeration to suggest that many West Indian planters wanted to use the now-banned whips to flog Wilberforce and his friends.

If 'one man's meat is another's poison', the news of the amelioration concessions was like a three course meal to enslaved Africans in the West Indies. In what is now Guyana, Africans believed Canning's reforms signified the end of slavery and imminent freedom. The colonial authorities, however, as stubborn as ever, quibbled about implementing these concessions, which Africans construed as a refusal to heed British demands. At Le Resouvenir, an estate in Demerara, British Guiana, Africans demanded immediate emancipation and killed two overseers who resisted them. Martial law was then declared and 100 rioters were killed.

Not for the first time, or the last, missionaries were blamed for the African uprisings. In Demerara, the chief culprit was reportedly the British missionary John Smith who was the pastor at the local Bethel Chapel. Smith had taken his missionary duties seriously and was known to have forged good relationships with his African congregation. He shared with them the discussions in London about amelioration and emancipation and it was this that brought him into conflict with the authorities.

After the riot, the Governor of Demerara instigated a crackdown on all missionary activity among Africans and had Pastor Smith arrested and imprisoned for seven weeks. Smith was to later be put on trial for sedition – the charges included telling enslaved Africans that the king had ordered the freeing of all slaves. Smith responded to these accusations by stating that he knew the British government had ordered the governor to make some changes, but that he had never told the Africans they were free. The Africans were asked to give evidence and most appeared to agree with Smith's version of events. However, the testimony of Africans rarely saved a person from the gallows, and the vengeful planters pressed for the death sentence. Smith was set to lodge an appeal to the Secretary of State for the Colonies when he died suddenly in prison – no doubt the strain of the case played a part in his demise. For the abolitionists back in Britain, Smith quickly became a martyr and his mistreatment typified the sheer stubbornness and cruelty underpinning slave societies, which were inflexible and unjust to both Africans and their white sympathizers alike.

The repercussions of Smith's arrest and trial went as far as the British parliament. Wilberforce's last appearances in the House of Commons in June 1824 were taken up with raising the Smith case with his fellow MPs. However, his call for an inquiry into the Smith scenario was rejected by MPs who were still more concerned about safeguarding the property interests of West Indian planters than a minor legal injustice. But to those whose work involved spreading the Christian gospel overseas, the Smith debacle served to highlight the barbaric, anti-Christian practices of some West Indian colonies. Christian abolitionist MPs used parliament to make representations on behalf of the Christian missionaries who were still being persecuted by the West Indian authorities after the Smith case. One of the most vocal of these critics was Thomas Fowell Buxton,* who took over the role as leader of the abolitionists in parliament in 1825 after Wilberforce's retirement. Buxton had helped to found the Society for the Mitigation and Gradual Abolition of Slavery and worked closely with Wilberforce to shape the amelioration concessions.

In fact, Buxton was a curious combination of Anglicanism and Quakerism. His father, also called Thomas, was a staunch Anglican while his mother and wife were Quakers and it was his maternal connections that stirred his initial interest in the slave trade. He was elected as a member of parliament for Weymouth in 1818 and, like Wilberforce, he was a Tory. However, his Quaker tendencies saw him take an interest in social reform and he would use his parliamentary position to work for an improvement in prison conditions, the end of capital punishment and the abolition of slavery.

---

* A tiny image of the bespectacled Buxton can be seen standing on the extreme left of the British five-pound note, which carries the portrait of Victorian reformer and friend of Buxton, Elizabeth Fry.

The retirement of Wilberforce heralded a sea change within the abolition movement. Women, who had previously been in the shadows, became more visible in anti-slavery activity during the 1820s. Akin to the previous generation of female abolitionists, the women from this era clearly identified with the plight of disenfranchised Africans and made 'sisterhood bonds' with enslaved African women. Historical studies show that African women largely bore the brunt of abuses throughout chattel enslavement – rape and other violations were common occurences on slave ships and plantations. Even pregnant women were beaten without impunity, and often overseers dug holes in the ground to accommodate their stomachs while they were stretched out for a flogging. Others were forced to work with their newborn babies strapped to their backs.

As the writer Vron Ware points out, abolitionist women's 'literature was often quite explicit about the "indecencies" that women slaves endured as they were stripped and beaten by male overseers. In doing so they identified the specific oppression of women slaves; either as objects of lust and brutality at the hands of white male overseers, or as victims of a system that denied them any kind of natural domestic existence'.[4]

One such female voice for emancipation was Elizabeth Heyrick, a Leicester-born Quaker convert. Heyrick's elder brother, Samuel, had been part of the original abolition movement in the 1790s, and she became interested in the campaign through his work. Heyrick was responsible for organizing slave-produced sugar boycotts in her native Leicester and she was also influential in the formation of the powerful Birmingham Ladies' Society for the Relief of Negro Slaves which later became the Female Society for Birmingham.

As well as calling for women to be part of the movement's leadership, Heyrick disseminated her progressive ideas in the

1824 pamphlet *Immediate not Gradual Abolition.* This seminal tract condemned slavery as sinful and called for the immediate freeing of enslaved Africans within the British dependencies.

However, *Immediate not Gradual Abolition* brought her into sharp conflict with the abolition movement, as her views ran contrary to the official policy which favoured amelioration or gradual abolition. Wilberforce, never a champion of women's involvement in the movement, tried his utmost to stifle knowledge of the pamphlet and instructed the movement's leaders not to speak at women's anti-slavery societies.

But despite Wilberforce's protestation, by the second half of the 1820s, towns and cities such as Nottingham, Sheffield, Norwich, Darlington, Chelmsford, London and Glasgow boasted 'Ladies' Associations' – as they were politely termed. By the start of the following decade, the number of associations had swelled to over 70 with virtually every region in Britain having a female abolition group.

There is little doubt that women abolitionists were more radical than their male counterparts. For example, in 1827 the Sheffield Female Society was the first group to appeal for the direct freedom of enslaved Africans. Women subsequently lobbied the main anti-slavery movement for a policy change, but with an absence of female representation among the leadership, their attempts failed. The women subsequently changed tack and decided to use their economic influence to change policies.

Under Heyrick's influence, the well-supported Female Society for Birmingham persuaded other Ladies' Associations to withdraw funding from the central committee. Heyrick's position was strengthened by the knowledge that women provided over a fifth of all the central committees' donations, yet she had to wait until 1830 to witness a significant change in the anti-slavery society's policy. It was that year that her society presented a motion to the Society for the Abolition of the Slave Trade's (formerly, the Committee for the Abolition of the African Slave Trade) National Conference demanding an immediate cessation of chattel enslavement. At the conference, the Society agreed to the women's demands to drop the word 'gradual' from its name and campaign instead for immediate abolition.

The Society for the Abolition of the Slave Trade was once again split between radicals wanting an immediate end to slavery and the more conventional elements who were still calling for gradual abolition. By the early 1830s, it appeared that the radicals were outflanking their opponents. Buoyed by their success within the Society, the radicals formed a subcommittee – or agency committee – which focused on slavery atrocities and re-emphasized its immoral activities. The agency committee employed researchers and speakers who toured Britain armed with information and statistics on the brutality of slavery. Once again, the Quakers proved an invaluable ally, providing the committee with funding and organizational savvy so that no area of Britain remained untouched in what the agency regarded clearly as the final push for abolition.

By the 1830s, Thomas Fowell Buxton was busily occupying Wilberforce's huge boots in parliament. Buxton was considered more radical than many on the issue of immediate emancipation, but radicals such as those on the agency committee regarded him as conformist. For the radicals, the gradualist or amelioration approach was neither 'fish nor fowl', holding out the tantalizing fruits of freedom to Africans but failing to deliver the goods. Even the West Indian planters disliked it because it created uncertainty within their industry. They were naturally against any overseas meddling in their affairs, but what they hated even more was the 'will they, won't they' approach to ending slavery. Some Jamaican and Barbadian planters and their cohorts in the respective Crown Colony Assemblies had contemplated seceding from Britain and allying themselves with the slave-owning states in the southern half of the United States if the British parliament agreed to outlaw slavery. West Indian planters and assembly members regarded parliament as a thorn in their side and dreaded all communications from London. As a result, many chose to dismiss all British law reforms, and it was this stubborn refusal to implement parliamentary legislation that created mayhem in Jamaica in 1831. Once more, Africans throughout the West Indies heard about events unfolding within parliament and interpreted their assemblies' rejection of certain reforms as a reluctance to set them free. In Jamaica, enslaved Africans took umbrage and initiated the greatest rebellion that the island experienced during slavery.

The Christmas Rebellion of 1831, as it became known, was arguably the event that drove the final nail into the coffin of the British West Indian slave industry. For planters and estate managers, it rammed home the unstable nature of West Indian slavery and their precarious existence as a white minority in a hostile, black dominated society. In Britain, the scale of the rebellion and the way in which it was quelled highlighted that no supporter of a civilized society could ever again advocate such an institution.

The events of 1831 had their roots in various socio-economic and political changes that were occurring at the time in most West Indian societies. By the 1820s, the demographic transformations in the ethnic composition of such societies saw the emergence of a sizeable free population. Many of the free individuals were the offspring of interracial relationships, while others were Africans who had purchased their freedom. This growing class had doubled to almost 12 per cent by the mid 1820s, at a time when the white population was in decline.

The new stratum, especially 'coloured' people, considered themselves West Indians with few allegiances to Britain. By 1823, societies for people of colour in Jamaica were demanding greater rights, such as voting and property rights, and the opportunity to play an improved role within civic society. By 1829, the people of colour (mulattos) had their own newspaper, *The Watchman*, which called for more rights for 'West Indians' – those whose allegiances were to the colonies and not the crown – as well as an end to slavery.

The composition of the enslaved African population had also undergone changes with the numbers of Africans born in the West Indies swelling to match those brought straight from Africa. These Creole (West Indian-born or 'seasoned') Africans spoke a *lingua franca* which had nullified previous attempts by planters to mix Africans of different languages in order to create disharmony. Moreover, although some local born Africans had never tasted personal freedom within Africa, slave societies still contained numerous Africans who had, and these people furnished their compatriots with tales of liberty back home in the mother country.

Religion also assisted in bringing about changes in society. Firstly, concerted religious activity by earnest missionaries within non-conformist denominations resulted in African deacons holding leadership roles in churches. Many of these Africans could read and write and relayed to their congregants an alternative interpretation of the scriptures that emphasized ideas of liberation, justice and equality. Unlike some of their white counterparts, African deacons were never reluctant to mix religion and practical ideas on African emancipation, and it was no coincidence that pastors such as Sam Sharpe, a Baptist deacon in Jamaica, and Quamina Gladstone, a pastor in Demerara, were central figures in the major West Indian insurrections of the 1820s and 30s.

Similarly, the non-Christian religions brought by the Africans also acted as a source of defiance and inspiration, although many Africans were forced to practise these secretly because most West Indian territories banned all non-Christian religious practices. They circumvented these restrictions by mixing in aspects of Christianity to make their religious practices appear acceptable to the authorities. This form of syncretism was particularly common in colonies which followed Roman Catholicism such as Haiti, the Dominican Republic, Puerto Rico, Brazil and Cuba. However, many different religions played a role in the slave-inspired uprisings and African-derived practices such as Obeah, Vodun (or as some call it, Voodoo), Candomblé and Lukumi were a vital source of inspiration and cohesion for Africans. For instance, Nanny, the female leader of the Jamaican Maroons who fought against the British, was said to possess supernatural powers due to the practice of Obeah which made her impervious to bullets. And prior to the Haitian or St Domingue Revolution, Toussaint L'Ouverture and his compatriots held a Vodun ceremony in which they swore to end French rule. It is also said that these Haitian freedom fighters were protected by a Vodun hex.

Religion was also central to the Jamaican uprising of 1831. Not only did it take place around one of the holiest dates in the Christian calendar, Christmas, but a Baptist preacher, Sam Sharpe, instigated it. Sharpe was a house slave whose masters had given him a degree of latitude in order to carry out mission work among his fellow enslaved Africans on the estates in the Parish of St James, in west Jamaica. By all accounts, Sharpe's surname reflected his intelligence – he read widely and possessed the leadership qualities to take up the role of deacon in the Burchell Baptist Church in Montego Bay, Jamaica's second city. The Wesleyan missionary to Jamaica, Revd H. Bleby, described Sharpe as the most remarkable and intelligent slave he had ever met.

Sharpe was also an advocate of emancipation and followed closely the abolition debates in Britain by reading discarded newspapers. He would subsequently relay this information back to his compatriots during Bible lessons and nightly religious meetings. Sharpe was soon convinced that the Jamaican planters were holding back on essential reforms and organized what we would now call a 'sit-down' protest together with his compatriots. At one of his religious meetings, he encouraged his compatriots to swear an oath on the Bible to withdraw their labour after Christmas Day 1831, until they were given better treatment and the planters were ready to discuss the issue of their emancipation. Congregants at that infamous night-time meeting departed to spread the news to around 50,000 enslaved Africans in the Jamaican parishes (counties) of Trelawny, Westmoreland, St Elizabeth and Manchester.

There is little doubt that Sharpe intended to achieve these aims through peaceful means; unfortunately for him, some Africans misinterpreted his message and believed it to be a call to arms. Conversely, when word of the 'sit-down' protest reached the ears of some of the Jamaican planters, troops were dispatched to St James and the Jamaican assembly also moored warships in Montego Bay with their weaponry trained on towns and villages. The situation came to a head a few days later when the Kensington Estate Great House in St James was set on fire, signalling the start of the rebellion. Over the following days, palatial houses and plantations throughout the west of the island were torched and it is estimated that 20,000 enslaved Africans were involved.[5]

When the militia finally managed to end the uprising, 14 whites and over 500 enslaved Africans had been killed. The authorities immediately wanted to make examples of the rebels to deter any further uprisings and Africans were rounded up on an *ad hoc* basis, regardless of whether they were involved in the rebellion. One of those accused of riotous sedition was Sam Sharpe.

Sharpe was tried in a kangaroo court and hanged on 23 May 1832 for his part as the rebellion's organizer. His last words, 'I would rather die in yonder gallows than live for a minute more in slavery', stand as a testimony to his belief that slavery was immoral and wicked.* Of the 634 enslaved Africans tried, almost half were sentenced to death by hanging and the rest were flogged for related crimes. The Rebellion's repercussions included gangs of militiamen enforcing summary justice on any African they deemed to have been involved in the uprising. There was also a clampdown on the missionaries in Jamaica who were seen as the root cause of the dissent. In addition, the Revd George Wilson Bridges established the Colonial Church Union, an Anglican-based militia group that worked to rid the island of its missionaries. Members of the Union were responsible for the destruction of 16 churches in various Jamaican parishes and the harassment and arrest of British missionaries such as the Baptists William Knibb and Thomas Burchell, the Moravian H.G. Pfeiffer and the Methodist Henry Whiteley.

William Knibb had arrived in Jamaica in 1824 and was instrumental in Sam Sharpe's emergence as a deacon and a spiritual leader. During the Christmas Rebellion of 1831, Knibb actually encouraged rebellious Africans to put down their weapons and return to their plantations. However, as he was a

* Sam Sharpe has been accorded 'National Hero' status in Jamaica. A square in Montego Bay, Jamaica's second city, is named after him and his image adorns the Jamaican $50 bill.

missionary, the Colonial Church Union saw him as an enemy. The Colonial Church Union soon discovered that it had an ally in the *Jamaica Courant*, a local newspaper, which ran an editorial on the missionaries soon after the uprising. In it they suggested, 'shooting is too honourable a death for these men whose conduct occasioned so much bloodshed, and the loss of so much property'.[6]

William Knibb was strongly encouraged to leave the island and his arrival in Britain in early 1832 coincided with much soul-searching about what could be done with the West Indies. Knibb wasted no time entering the debate and embarked on a nationwide speaking tour on which he railed against the violence of the Jamaican authorities in relation to the aftermath of the Jamaica Rebellion. Knibb also used the Rebellion as a platform to condemn West Indian slavery as a whole and its obvious cruelty towards Africans, providing first-hand descriptions of the nastiness of the overseers and estate managers towards Africans. As neither Buxton nor any of the other leading abolitionists had visited the West Indies, Knibb's testimony gave real credibility and added urgency to the anti-slavery cause. Henry Whiteley, who was also exiled from Jamaica for his missionary activities, assisted Knibb with the publication of the book *Three Months in Jamaica*, a best-selling account of his time on the island that also focused attention on the need for immediate rather than gradual emancipation.

West Indian planters obviously could not dismiss these first-hand accounts as the fanciful tales of folk who knew nothing about the realities of West Indian slavery. However, they did send depositions to parliament to promote the view that the full liberation of Africans would lead to utter chaos, while also pointing to the actions of Sam Sharpe, who they blamed for turning a would-be strike into a mass riot. They solicited parliament for support in quelling any future uprisings, as they feared any such activity would result in the collapse of their economies and lead to bankruptcy for the colonies. In 1832, ever concerned with the maintenance of property, the British government voted to give £200,000 to help restore the properties of Jamaican planters.

The abolitionists soon received a fillip in the form of the British parliamentary reforms of 1832, which saw a widening of the franchise to include the rising numbers of middle class voters. The Great Reform Act of June 1832 created a new wave of MPs with fewer loyalties to the sugar and slavery lobbies, who were more sympathetic to the abolitionists' cause. Moreover, many of these newly-elected MPs had constituencies in cities such as Manchester and Birmingham, traditionally strongholds of the abolitionist movement.

The abolitionists largely welcomed the Reform Act, as MPs such as Wilberforce and Buxton were aware that changes were needed to rid parliament of some of its more corrupt practices. And yet, in May 1832, while the Reform debates were in their final stages, Buxton chose to introduce a motion before the Commons for the total freedom of enslaved Africans. Buxton knew that the government would be against his motion, which, if brought to a vote, could possibly bring down the Whig Administration, thus destroying the parliamentary reform legislation. Buxton's many friends as well as his increasing number of enemies encouraged him to either remove or water down his motion to ensure that no damage was done to the Reform Bill. However, Buxton stood his ground; as a principled man he believed parliamentary unpopularity was suitable compensation for the freeing of the Africans in the West Indies. His subsequent bill, which was defeated by 136 votes to 92, did not result in the collapse of the government, but clearly showed the increasing strength of the abolitionists within parliament. Even those who had voted against the bill were cognisant that the days of West Indian slavery were clearly numbered and moved to protect the interests of West Indian planters when this eventually occurred.

The defeat of Buxton's parliamentary efforts spurred the Ladies' Associations into sending the single largest petition of women's signatures – some 187,000 – to parliament to protest at its growing intransigence to ending slavery. Faith groups were also aghast at the lack of parliamentary activity and according to the historian Robin Blackburn, Methodist congregations were responsible for sending parliament more than 1,900 petitions. Other clergymen used more imaginative ways of protesting such as parading up and down Downing Street in their full clerical regalia.

By early 1833, the slavery issue had become the primary political concern in Britain and other anti-slavery pressure groups presented petitions, containing hundreds of thousands of signatures, declaring that parliament was again out of step with public opinion. A clear sign of this gulf was the king's speech at the opening of parliament in February 1833, which failed to cite any business on slavery. The Prime Minister, Lord Grey, under pressure from Buxton, was then forced to introduce parliamentary legislation that addressed the slavery question. For Buxton the issue was simple: the government should recommend a scheme for the ending of slavery and propose a date by which it should happen. By May 1833, the government had recognized that the amelioration argument was a failing one and it had to consider quickly what would happen when, rather than if, abolition occurred.

As before, the government's primary concerns lay with the West Indian planters. It was worried that if it freed the Africans, they would abandon the plantations, resulting in the bankruptcy of planters. With this in mind, it devised a financial package for the planters to compensate for 'hardships' such as the potential loss of labour and income.

To further reinforce its commitment to the planters, the government also suggested an 'apprenticeship' scheme for the enslaved Africans, acting as a 'halfway house' between enslavement and freedom. It was sold to the abolitionists as an opportunity for the enslaved Africans to come to terms with 'the dynamics of freedom', but in reality it was an opportunity for planters to continue to utilize Africans on their plantations, therefore alleviating any loss of labour. Under the proposed apprenticeship scheme, Africans were required to work 'three quarters of their time for their existing masters for a period of twelve years'. And to further compensate for the loss of a quarter of the slaves' labour time, parliament agreed to loan the planters £15 million.

As with all political horse-trading, Buxton and the other abolitionist MPs both won and lost concessions. Although they persuaded the government to reduce the apprenticeship period by half from twelve to six years, they could not stop the upping of the planters' compensation from £15 to £20 million. Moreover, the £20 million would no longer be a loan, but a gift that was equal to 40 per cent of the national budget.[7] This princely sum was the cause of much letter writing and cartoon drawing in the British Press. West Indian planters were known for their wealth and it was claimed that it was wrong to bankrupt the country in order to compensate these already prosperous individuals. Others argued that if anyone should receive monies, it ought to be the Africans themselves. Buxton was denounced as unprincipled for allowing the planters to receive such huge amounts of compensation, and cowardly for caving into parliament by failing to secure funds for Africans.

The Emancipation Bill (or Bill for the Total Abolition of Colonial Slavery) was passed in both houses of parliament in the summer of 1833. Slavery in the British colonies would officially end the following year, on 31 July 1834. There was even less of a fanfare than in 1807, however, because everyone knew, to coin a phrase from the television advert, that it did not do exactly 'what it says on the tin'. Under the apprenticeship scheme, Africans were forced to work for their masters for another six years. Only children under six experienced a significant transformation in their status and were fully free. However, being so young, they were probably unaware of the significance of what had happened to them.

10

New Beginnings

One of the reasons for parliament's reluctance to end West Indian slavery was the fear of an African-inspired massacre of whites, on a scale of Haiti, after emancipation. As a consequence, the period between 31 July 1833 (the date when the Emancipation Bill was passed) and 1 August 1834 (the date when the Act came into effect) was a worrying time for the British colonial office. Not everyone shared their concerns, and in Britain, Thomas Fowell Buxton was personally congratulated for his hard work in the campaign. However, many thoughts were with William Wilberforce who had died earlier that summer on 29 July. Although massively incapacitated by illness, he continued to take an active interest in the abolition movement right up until the end.

As it was, there were no massacres in 1834 when slavery gave way to apprenticeship, and it was soon business as usual. The apprenticeship system was adopted by all the West Indian colonies except for Antigua. In Britain, Christians marked this event with thanksgiving services and some celebrated the date as Liberation Day. Buxton was given a silver plate by his relatives to acknowledge his invaluable contribution.

While Britain was celebrating, however, joy in the West Indies soon turned to sorrow when the reality of apprenticeship dawned on the Africans. The historian Matheson pointed out that '… on 1 August 1834 slave masters and freed slaves rejoiced together at religious services and how, on Monday following, the freed slaves found that the planters had combined to set a fixed daily wage of one shilling for skilled workers and nine pence for others'. He continues, 'The Act which abolished slavery did not emancipate the slaves... As a social institution slavery disappeared... and it came back as a system of industry, the Negroes... having to work as slaves for so many hours a week.'[1]

Apprenticeship was slavery in all but name, and both the abolitionists and the British government soon began receiving reports confirming this. It seems that old habits died hard: many an overseer or estate manager wanted their African labourers to work more than the agreed nine hours a day, and would argue over the food allowance given to apprentices. The social systems and structures established during slavery were also still left in place, making it impossible for Africans to thrive as free men and women. Africans were excluded from many sections of West Indian society because of their ethnicity and were denied any official representation.

On many of the smaller islands, the planters owned so much land that Africans were forced to go back to their old masters and carry out the same work, in similar conditions as before. In some instances, Africans were materially worse off after slavery due to the apprenticeship system. Under slavery, they were not financially responsible for finding food or a place to live for themselves or their families, but the pittance they received as apprentices could not meet these new financial concerns.

On larger islands or territories where land was available, the former enslaved Africans pooled together their resources to form what became known as 'free villages', which enabled some degree of self-sufficiency. These free villages were similar to the settlements established by runaway enslaved Africans (Maroon towns) before emancipation, but were given greater encouragement once they were free. In Jamaica, the church was responsible for the establishment of numerous free villages after 1833, which enabled the 'growth of the peasant proprietors or freeholders'.[2]

The Quaker abolitionist Joseph Sturge was one man who had doubted from the outset the worth of the apprenticeship scheme. When he heard reports of abuse and material poverty in the West Indies, he did what very few abolitionists achieved during slavery, namely to visit the area himself. Accompanied by his colleague Thomas Harvey, he visited various West Indian islands to assess what was really taking place during apprenticeship. He found that in Antigua, which had never opted for apprenticeship, the economic and social conditions of the Africans were far better than in Jamaica, which had.

During his stay in Jamaica, he worked with William Knibb, who had returned to the island from Britain to help 500 families settle on 500 acres of land and establish the village of Sturge Town, which included a church and school. On his return to Britain, Sturge completed the publication *The West Indies in 1837*, published in 1838, which 'exposed for a broad public the cruelty and injustice of apprenticeship'. He also brought over Jamaicans who railed against the systems' inadequacies and injustices.

Sturge's work galvanized those keen to see an end of this pseudo slavery. The abolitionists produced iconic posters showing a version of the Wedgwood anti-slavery figure with the words, 'Englishmen! Negro Apprenticeship is proved to be but another name for slavery.' Petitions were also sent to parliament and speeches took place in towns and cities in order to fully confine West Indian slavery to the annals of history. Knibb remained busy in Jamaica at this time and regularly sent reports back to Buxton, highlighting new abuses within the apprenticeship system.

The numerous petitions and the almost daily accounts of mistreatment coming from the West Indies forced parliament's hand, bringing an early end to apprenticeship. The government took steps to end the system by the summer of 1838, just four years after it was introduced. The colonies agreed to this and the real freedom celebrations in the West Indies took place on 1 August 1838, when all Africans could finally call themselves 'fully free'.*

In Jamaica, Knibb officiated over a symbolic 'burying of the chains', presiding over a thanksgiving service in his church with its walls hung with portraits of Clarkson and Wilberforce. In a coffin, inscribed "Colonial Slavery, died July 31 1838, aged 276", church members placed an iron punishment collar, whip and chains. The coffin was subsequently 'exhumed' and the chains are now to be found in a presentation case outside the General Secretary of the Baptist Union of Great Britain offices in Didcot, Oxfordshire.

After 1838, emancipated Africans in the larger West Indian territories such as British Guiana, Trinidad and Jamaica left the plantations en masse to establish free villages. The colonial authorities agreed to meet this labour deficit by encouraging the West Indian planters to seek labourers from Europe. Once again, indentured labour was reintroduced to the West Indies with Portuguese workers from Madeira coming to islands such as Trinidad on five-year contracts. Jamaica received British and German labourers a few years later.

These indentured labourers were largely unused to agricultural tasks and disliked the thought of carrying out work formerly done by Africans. Many abandoned the countryside as soon as their contracts expired, preferring other professions

---

* 1 August 1838 is now known as Emancipation Day, an annual holiday throughout the former British West Indies.

'more worthy' of their race. Some never acclimatized to the monotony of the seasons or the heat of the West Indies and returned home. Such was the chronic shortage of workers on islands such as Jamaica that the colonial governors and the West Indian planters soon persuaded the British government to introduce immigration from West Africa, much to the mortification of missionaries in Sierra Leone. By and large, however, these Africans were reluctant to leave their country because the labour system proposed by the British resembled slavery.

By far the largest form of immigration came in the shape of indentured labour from the Asian subcontinent, where Indians (usually called East Indians in the West Indies) arrived in their thousands after the real ending of slavery in 1838. In places such as British Guiana, Trinidad and Jamaica, they worked on the sugar plantations on five or ten-year contracts and such was the sustained nature of this form of contractual labour that the demography of many West Indian territories was drastically altered.*

By 1838, only Thomas Clarkson was left of the original British nucleus of the 1787 abolitionists to witness real African freedom from West Indian slavery. Clarkson was approaching 80 and in failing health (his eyesight had almost gone), yet he was still to be found campaigning against the remnants of slavery in Africa and other parts of the world. He would play a key role in establishing the British and Foreign Anti-Slavery Society, which was formed on 17 April 1839, and which is now known as Anti-Slavery International.

Rather than being able to rest in his dotage, however, he was

---

* In Guyana (formerly British Guiana), East Indians make up half of the country's current population, while in Trinidad, the East Indian population forms around a third of the nation's populace.

forced to defend himself against the accusations made in a book written by the sons of his old friend, William Wilberforce. To mark the real ending of slavery, Wilberforce's sons produced *Life of William Wilberforce*, their account of Wilberforce senior's involvement in the abolition movement, and much like Clarkson's version of 1808, it was very one-sided. Some argued that it was the Wilberforce family's opportunity to get their own back on Clarkson, whose own account had clearly embellished his role in ending the slave trade while downplaying Wilberforce's.

If Clarkson's account smacked of selective amnesia, the Wilberforce account was downright nasty, accusing Clarkson of everything from being a 'hired hand' to being the person who 'frustrated and delayed all attempts at abolition'. The book's publication deeply distressed Clarkson and no doubt would have had William Wilberforce turning in his grave. Although he and Clarkson always had differences, Wilberforce had the utmost respect and admiration for his colleague in the fight against slavery and would not have wanted to see him so savagely attacked in print. Wilberforce's sons did eventually see the error of their ways and apologized to Clarkson in 1844, two years before his death.

But for all his hard work in helping to end the slave trade and slavery, Clarkson is now one of the forgotten men of history. It would be true to argue that today, politicians, Christian evangelicals and 'the establishment' cleave to William Wilberforce as the one who epitomized all that was – and is – good about the British commitment to justice and decency. Wilberforce remains the key figure of the abolition movement and many people's knowledge of slavery starts and ends with him. Those wanting an alternative figure to show another side of the freedom movement look to Olaudah Equiano. Those of African ancestry especially identify with him, seeing him as a gallant figure who battled against race, class and cultural prejudice in order to write his autobiography and help to end slavery. Thomas Clarkson, however, falls between two stools. Up until now, there have been very few books or documentaries on his life and it is ironic that the second edition of *The Cambridge Encyclopedia*, which has close links to Cambridge University, Clarkson's *alma mater*, has no entry for him, yet it does have one for William Wilberforce.

The abolition of slavery in the British colonies also proved to be the stimulus for other European countries to examine the preservation of the labour system in their colonies. Yet, with the exception of France and Holland, during the nineteenth century the other historic European slaving nations were rapidly losing control of their colonies in the Americas and were in no position to influence the ending of slavery. Portugal lost control of its South American jewel, Brazil, by the 1820s, while Spain would experience similar problems during the South American independence movement, led by 'the liberator' Simón Bolívar. As with Britain and the United States, or France and Haiti, by the 1830s Spain and Portugal could not force their former territories to free their enslaved Africans. As a result of independence, these American countries pursued their own economic paths and chose to end slavery when it suited them.

The French would end West Indian slavery in Martinique, Guadeloupe and French Guiana in 1848. Slavery came to an end in the United States in 1865 as a result of the American civil war, which was, ultimately, a power struggle between the industrialized Northern States and the slave-owning Confederacy in the South. War was also the primary reason for the abolition of slavery in Cuba. The enslaved Africans who fought in the Ten Years' War (1868–78) were promised their freedom if they sided with the Cuban compatriots against

Spain. Spain would eventually abolish slavery in 1886. Brazil, perhaps the greatest slave-receiving nation of them all, would finally end African slavery in 1888.

Brazil's decision to end slavery, some 50 years after Britain's ending of slavery in her colonies, brought an official end to slavery in the Americas. Throughout the area, African people struggled to shake off the legacy of centuries of slavery and began new battles for civil rights, respect and dignity from the whites who would continue to exclude them from society. The countries in the West Indies would become part of Britain's empire, while all Spanish, Dutch and Danish territories would fall under the United States' sphere of influence.

In Africa, the ending of chattel enslavement in the British colonies heralded a scramble for Africa. With the exception of Belgium, the rush to colonize and 'civilize' the vast continent was primarily led by the major European slaving nations, who already had toeholds along the West African coastline because of their previous involvement in slave trading. Studies today reveal that certain European countries used the pretext of ending all slavery within Africa to justify their exploitation of the continent's resources.

Others took up what Rudyard Kipling would later call 'The White Man's Burden', and carved up large sections of the continent, drawing boundaries where none had previously existed, and paying little or no attention to the customs, cultures or religious practices of the people already living there. The after-effects of such a myopic approach to colonization are still being felt in Africa today.

This book is not the right place to start this particular debate, but the bicentenary of the Abolition of the Slave Trade Act should be a moment to assess the real contribution of Africa and its people to the development of the West and assess whether that involuntary involvement can ever be repaid. Issues of trade and underdevelopment in Africa continue to focus many minds in the West, and one has to be ask whether the roots of the trade inequalities, stunted development and sheer chauvinism with regard to Africa are directly traceable to the Transatlantic Slave Trade. The last point is a moot one among many African heritage groups in Britain who believe that the West has always patronized Africa, first during colonialism, and much later through trade and aid issues. These groups also argue that the West often excludes Africans from discussions about the continent's future, believing that they have all the solutions to the 'African problem'. A clear example of this 'about us, without us' scenario was the G8 Gleneagles Summit in July 2005, where African leaders were invited to the discussion only after the West's leaders had already sorted out its future. It can be argued that it would be inconceivable to have a summit on the Middle East and exclude Arab or Israeli delegates, or have discussions on the future of Northern Ireland and not invite Loyalist or Republican representatives.

The bicentenary of the Abolition of the Transatlantic Slave Trade helped to underline the fact that part of the reason why worldwide enslavement continues today is society's reluctance to talk about slavery. Unlike the Holocaust, which was also one of the most tragic episodes in history, slavery does not have a similar commemoration day in Britain. This denies people the opportunity to delve into what took place and find out more about modern examples of mistreatment, prejudice and murder. As a consequence, few in Britain today have a good working knowledge of the Transatlantic Slave Trade and even fewer are aware of the issues surrounding modern-day slavery. The bicentenary, therefore, is an occasion for men and women of all ethnicities and religions, in the spirit of the original abolitionists, to work together to end the negative legacies of slavery, as well as commit themselves to ending modern-day slavery.

Sources

The genesis of this book began in the late 1980s, when as a student, I carried out extensive research on slavery in Britain and overseas while studying for my first degree. The information I amassed was supplemented by material from libraries, institutes and information centres from across the world.

In London, I spent time at London Metropolitan University (formerly North London University), Queen Mary College, the Black Cultural Archives, the Africa Centre, the Institute of Commonwealth Studies and the British Library. I also used the parliamentary archives of the United Kingdom which provided access to material relating to slavery legislation. I would like to extend personal thanks to David Irwin at the Religious Society of Friends Library in Euston, London, and Jeff Howarth, librarian at Anti-Slavery International in Stockwell, South London.

During the late 1980s and 1990s, I regularly visited Jamaica and made use of the facilities and resources of the Institute of Jamaica and the offices of the *Gleaner* newspaper in Kingston. I also frequented the library at the University of the West Indies at the Mona Heights Campus in uptown Kingston.

I paid a visit to Gambia to assess the impact of the slave trade on that country and to find out more about my roots. I am grateful for the friends who provided me with much-needed information and resources that have helped in the compilation of this book.

I also used the facilities at the University of Andres Bello in Caracas, Venezuela, and the Museo Histórico de Guanabacoa in Havana, Cuba, during visits to those respective countries. I am grateful for the hospitality and generosity extended to me by colleagues in the Pelourinho district of the city of Salvador in north-eastern Brazil. Brazil was one of the key slave reception centres for enslaved Africans and Salvador has several historical sites and museums connected to the Transatlantic Slave Trade.

I am also thankful to the staff at the Schomburg Center for Research in Black Culture in New York, whose assistance and patience helped me during my initial research in 2005.

Endnotes

Introduction

1 Leary, Joy DeGruy, *Post-Traumatic Slave Syndrome: America's Legacy of Enduring Injury and Healing*, Uptone Press, 2005.

2 Hamilton, Alan, 'If only Britain had thought of something like the Magna Carta', *The Times*, 30 May 2006.

3 Gregory, Philippa, *A Respectable Trade*, Harper Collins, 1996.

Chapter 1

1 Walter Rodney argued that the slave trade affected Africa negatively by causing depopulation, redirecting African's dynamism away from useful activities and fastening Africa into a sub-standard relationship with Europe that obstructed its industrial and economic development. (See: Rodney, Walter, *How Europe Underdeveloped Africa*, Bogle L'Ouverture. 1972.) David Eltis disagreed with Rodney's analysis of the economic effects on Africa and argued that Europe did not foist worthless products on Africans. Likewise, he suggested that European products did not undermine or undercut their African equivalents, and that African trade with Europe up until the nineteenth century was too small to generate a dependency culture. (See: Eltis, David, *Precolonial Western Africa and the Atlantic Economy* in *Slavery and the Rise of the Atlantic System*, edited by Barbara Solow, 1991.)

2 Davidson, Basil, *Africa in History: Themes and Outlines*, Paladin Books, 1974.

3 Diop, Cheikh Anta, *Pre-colonial Black Africa*, Lawrence Hill Books, 1987.

4 Diop, Cheikh Anta, *Pre-colonial Black Africa*, Lawrence Hill Books, 1987.

5 Davidson, Basil, *The Lost Cities of Africa*, Back Bay Books, 1988.

6 Battuta, Ibn, (Allah, Mohammed Ibn), *Travels in Asia and Africa*, translated by H.A.R. Gibb, 1929. Written in 1356.

7 Malouf, Amin, *Leo the African*, Abacus Books. 1994.

8 Dapper, Olfert, *Olfert Dapper's Description of Benin*, University of Wisconsin-Madison, 1998. Written in 1668.

9 Barbosa, Duarte, *Description of the Coasts of East Africa and Malabar*, Asian Educational Services, 1996.

10 Diaz del Castillo, Bernal, *The Conquest of New Spain*, translated with an introduction by J.M. Cohen, Penguin Books, 1963.

11 Davidson, Basil, *The Lost Cities of Africa*, Back Bay Books, 1988.

12 Williams, Eric, *Capitalism and Slavery*, Andre Deutsch, 1964.

13 Jordan, Winthrop D., *White over Black: American Attitudes Toward the Negro 1550–1812*, University of North Carolina, 1968.

14 Brady, Terence and Jones, Evan, *The Fight Against Slavery*, BBC Books, 1975.

15 Davis, David Brion, *Slavery and Human Progress*, Oxford University Press, 1984.

16 St Clair, William, *The Grand Slave Emporium: Cape Coast Castle and the British Slave Trade*, Profile Books, 2006.

17 St Clair, William, *The Grand Slave Emporium: Cape Coast Castle and the British Slave Trade*, Profile Books, 2006.

Chapter 2

1 Cameron, Gail and Crooke, Stan, *Liverpool – Capital of the Slave Trade*, Picton Press, 1992.

2 Many scholars now argue that there is significant evidence that Scandinavians and Africans reached the Americas centuries before Columbus. The Guyanese-born academic Ivan Van Sertima wrote the influential *They Came Before Columbus*, which explored the socio-cultural and religious similarities between Africa and the Americas. He concluded that Africans made voyages to the Americas in pre-Columbian times and left an indelible mark on civilizations there. Also, in *Black Discovery of America*, Canadian author Michael Bradley discusses similar themes. (See: Van Sertima, Ivan, *They Came Before Columbus: The African Presence in Ancient America*, Random House, 1976. Also, Bradley, Michael, *The Black Discovery of America: Amazing Evidence of Daring Voyages by Ancient West African Mariners*, Personal Library, 1981.)

3 Williams, Eric, *Capitalism and Slavery*, Andre Deutsch, 1964.

4 Heuman, Gad, *The Caribbean*, Hodder Arnold, 2006.

5 Equiano, Olaudah, *Equiano's Travels*, edited by Paul Edwards, Heinemann. 1967.

Chapter 3

1 Ogunde, Professor S.E., in the introduction to the *New Edition of Equiano's Travels*, Heinemann, 1997.

2 Segal, Ronald, *Islam's Black Slaves: the History of Africa's Other Black Diaspora*, Atlantic Books, 2001.

3 Segal, Ronald, *Islam's Black Slaves: the History of Africa's Other Black Diaspora*, Atlantic Books, 2001.

4 Equiano, Olaudah, *Equiano's Travels*, edited by Paul Edwards, Heinemann. 1967.

5 Clarkson, Thomas, *History of the Rise, Progress and Accomplishment of the Abolition of the African Slave Trade*, Longman, Hurst, Rees, and Orme, 1808.

6 Cugoano, Ottobah, quoted in Richard Hart's *Slaves Who Abolished Slavery: Volume I – Blacks in Bondage*, University of the West Indies Press, 1980.

7 Diouf, Sylviane A. (ed.), *Fighting the Slave Trade: West African Strategies*, James Currey Publishers, 2004.

8 Hart, Richard, *Slaves Who Abolished Slavery: Volume I – Blacks in Bondage*, University of the West Indies Press, 1980.

9 Hart, Richard, *Slaves Who Abolished Slavery: Volume I – Blacks in Bondage*, University of the West Indies Press, 1980.

10 Klein, Herbert S., *The Atlantic Trade*, Cambridge University Press, 1999.

11 Klein, Herbert S., *The Atlantic Trade*, Cambridge University Press, 1999.

12 Inikori, Joseph E., *Africans and the Industrial Revolution in England: A Study in International Trade and Economic Development*, University of Rochester, 2002.

13 Klein, Herbert S., *The Atlantic Trade*, Cambridge University Press, 1999.

14 Equiano, Olaudah, *Equiano's Travels*, edited by Paul Edwards, Heinemann, 1967.

15 Parry, J.H., Sherlock, Philip and Maingot, Anthony, *A Short History of the West Indies*, Macmillan, 1987.

16 Smith, M.G., *The Plural Society in the British West Indies*, University of California Press, 1974.

17 Augier, F.R. et al, *The Making of the West Indies*, Longman Caribbean, 1960.

18 Brady, Terence and Jones, Evan, *The Fight Against Slavery*, BBC Books, 1975.

Chapter 4

1 St Clair, William, *The Grand Slave Emporium: Cape Coast Castle and the British Slave Trade*, Profile Books, 2006.

Chapter 5

1 Gondola, Didier, *The History of Congo*, Greenwood Press, 2002.

2 James, C.L.R., *The Black Jacobins: Toussaint L'Ouverture and the San Domingo Revolution*, Alison & Busby, 1938.

3 Hayward, Jack (ed.), *Out of Slavery – Abolition and After: Legacies of West Indian Slavery*, Frank Cass, 1985.

Chapter 6

1 Smith, Adam, *An Inquiry into the Nature and Causes of the Wealth of Nations*, edited by Edwin Cannan, Random House, 1994.

2 Kohn, Marek, *The Race Gallery: the Return of Racial Science*, Jonathan Cape, 1995.

3 Long, Edward, *The History of Jamaica*, Ian Randle, 2003.

4 Tomkins, Stephen, *John Wesley: a Biography*, Lion, 2003.

5 Briggs, Asa, *England in the Age of Improvement: 1783–1867*, Folio Society, 1997.

6 Briggs, Asa, *England in the Age of Improvement: 1783–1867*, Folio Society, 1997.

Chapter 7

1 The American academic, Vincent Carretta, has argued that there is evidence to suggest that Equiano was born in South Carolina in North America and not Nigeria. Carretta has argued that Equiano's early accounts of his life in Africa were

241

borrowed from other sources. His later life experiences are said to be genuine. Carretta, Vincent, *Equiano the African: Biography of a Self-made Man*, University of Georgia, 2005.

2 Hill, Christopher, *Reformation to Industrial Revolution, Volume II: 1530–1780*, Penguin Books, 1969.

3 Ramsay, James, *An Essay on the Treatment and Conversion of African Slaves in the British Sugar Colonies*, J. Phillips, 1784.

4 Gifford, Zerbanoo, *Thomas Clarkson and the Campaign Against Slavery*, Anti-Slavery International, 1996.

5 Ephesians 6:9, New International Version, International Bible Society, 1984.

6 Augier, F.R. et al., *The Making of the West Indies*, Longman Caribbean, 1960.

7 Brady, Terence and Jones, Evan, *The Fight Against Slavery*, BBC Books, 1975.

8 Williams, Eric, *Capitalism and Slavery*, Andre Deutsch, 1964.

9 Clarkson, Thomas, *History of the Rise, Progress and Accomplishment of the Abolition of the African Slave Trade*, Longman, Hurst, Rees, and Orme, 1808.

10 Schama, Simon, *Rough Crossings: Britain, the Slaves and the American Revolution*, BBC Books, 2005.

11 Schama, Simon, *Rough Crossings: Britain, the Slaves and the American Revolution*, BBC Books, 2005.

12 Fryer, Peter, *Staying Power: History of Black People in Britain*, Pluto Press, 1984.

13 Barclay, Oliver, *Thomas Fowell Buxton and the Liberation of Slaves*, William Sessions Limited, 2001.

14 Clarkson, Thomas, *History of the Rise, Progress and Accomplishment of the Abolition of the African Slave Trade*, Longman, Hurst, Rees, and Orme, 1808.

15 Clarkson, Thomas, *History of the Rise, Progress and Accomplishment of the Abolition of the African Slave Trade*, Longman, Hurst, Rees, and Orme, 1808.

Chapter 8

1 Schama, Simon, *Rough Crossings: Britain, the Slaves and the American Revolution*, BBC Books, 2005.

2 Clarkson, Thomas, *History of the Rise, Progress and Accomplishment of the Abolition of the African Slave Trade*, Longman, Hurst, Rees, and Orme, 1808.

3 Clarkson, Thomas, *History of the Rise, Progress and Accomplishment of the Abolition of the African Slave Trade*, Longman, Hurst, Rees, and Orme, 1808.

4 Hobsbawm, Eric, *Industry and Empire: From 1750 to the Present Day*, Penguin, 1968.

5 Ware, Vron, *Beyond the Pale: White Women, Racism and History*, Verso, 1992.

6 Midgley, Clare, *Women Against Slavery: The British Campaigns 1780–1870*, Routledge, 1992.

7 *Manchester Mercury*. 6 November 1787.

8 Wollstonecraft, Mary, *A Vindication of the Rights of Woman*, Cambridge University Press, 1995.

9 Colley, Linda, *Britons: Forging the Nation 1707–1837*, Vintage, 1992.

10 Scott, Anne, *Hannah More: The First Victorian*, Oxford University Press, 2003.
11 Colley, Linda, *Britons: Forging the Nation 1707–1837*, Vintage, 1992.
12 Cobbett, William, *Cobbett's England: A Selection from the Writings of William Cobbett*, The Folio Society, 1968.

Chapter 9

1 Parry, J.H., Sherlock, Philip and Maingot, Anthony, *A Short History of the West Indies*, Macmillan, 1987.
2 Perez Jnr, Louis A., *Cuba: Between Reform and Revolution*, Oxford University Press, 1988.
3 Geggus, David, *Slave Resistance Studies and the Saint Domingue Slave Revolt: Some Preliminary Considerations*, Florida International University, 1983.
4 Ware, Vron, *Beyond the Pale: White Women, Racism and History*, Verso, 1992.
5 Heuman, Gad, *The Caribbean*, Hodder Arnold, 2006.
6 Brady, Terence and Jones, Evan, *The Fight Against Slavery*, BBC Books, 1975.
7 Hochschild, Adam, *Bury the Chains: The British Struggle to Abolish Slavery*, Macmillan, 2005.

Chapter 10

1 Parry, J.H., Sherlock, Philip and Maingot, Anthony, *A Short History of the West Indies*, Macmillan, 1987.
2 Black, Clinton V., *History of Jamaica*, Collins Press, 1973.

Selective Bibliography

Anstey, Roger, *The Atlantic Slave Trade and British Abolition, 1760–1810*, Macmillan, 1975.

Anta Diop, Cheikh, *Pre-colonial Black Africa*, Lawrence Hill Books, 1987.

Aughton, Peter, *Bristol: A People's History*, Carnegie Publishing, 2000.

Augier, F.R. et al, *The Making of the West Indies*, Longman Caribbean, 1960.

Bales, Kevin, *Understanding Global Slavery: A Reader*, University of California Press, 2005.

Barbosa, Duarte, *Description of the Coasts of East Africa and Malabar*, Asian Educational Services, 1996.

Barclay, Oliver, *Thomas Fowell Buxton and the Liberation of Slaves*, William Sessions Limited, 2001.

Battuta, Ibn, (Allah, Mohammed Ibn), *Travels in Asia and Africa*, 1929.

Black, Clinton V., *History of Jamaica*, Collins Press, 1973.

Blackburn, Robin, *The Overthrow of Colonial Slavery 1776–1848*, Verso, 1988.

Bradley, Michael, *The Black Discovery of America: Amazing Evidence of Daring Voyages by Ancient West African Mariners*, Personal Library, 1981.

Brady, Terence and Jones, Evan, *The Fight Against Slavery*, BBC books, 1975.

Bryant, Margaret, *The Clapham Sect*, The Clapham Society, 2004.

Briggs, Asa, *England in the Age of Improvement: 1783–1867*, The Folio Society, 1997.

Cameron, Gail and Crooke, Stan, *Liverpool – Capital of the Slave Trade*, Picton Press, 1992.

Canot, Theodore, *Adventures of an African slaver*, Dover, 1969.

Carretta, Vincent, *Equiano the African: Biography of a Self-made Man*, University of Georgia, 2005.

Clarkson, Thomas, *History of the Rise, Progress and Accomplishment of the Abolition of the African Slave Trade*, Longman, Hurst, Rees and Orme, 1808.

Cobbett, William, *Cobbett's England: A Selection from the Writings of William Cobbett*, The Folio Society, 1968.

Colley, Linda, *Britons: Forging the Nation 1707–1837*, Vintage, 1992.

Cone, James H., *The Spirituals and the Blues*, Orbis Books, 1998.

Costello, Ray, *Black Liverpool: the Early History of Britain's Oldest Black Community 1730–1918*, Picton Press. 2001.

Crossley Evans. M.J., *Hannah More*, No. 99, Local History Pamphlets, 1999.

Curtin, Philip D., *The Atlantic Slave Trade: A Census*, University of Wisconsin Press, 1969.

Dapper, Olfert, *Olfert Dapper's Description of Benin*, University of Wisconsin-Madison, 1998.

Davidson, Basil, *Africa in History: Themes and Outlines*, Paladin Books, 1974.

Davidson, Basil, *The Lost Cities of Africa*, Back Bay Books, 1988.

Davis, David Brion, *Inhuman Bondage: The Rise and Fall of Slavery in the New World*, Oxford University Press, 2005.

Davis, David Brion, *Slavery and Human Progress*, Oxford University Press, 1984.

DeGruy Leary, Joy, *Post-Traumatic Slave Syndrome: America's Legacy of Enduring Injury and Healing*, Uptone Press, 2005.

Diaz del Castillo, Bernal, *The Conquest of New Spain*, translated with an introduction by J.M. Cohen, Penguin Books, 1963.

Diop, Cheikh Anta, *Pre-colonial Black Africa*, Lawrence Hill Books, 1987.

Diouf, Sylviane A. (ed.), *Fighting the Slave Trade: West African Strategies*, James Currey Publishers, 2004.

Dookhan, Isaac, *A Post Emancipation History of the West Indies*, Longman Caribbean, 1975.

Drescher, Seymour, *The Mighty Experiment. Free Labour versus Slavery in British Emancipation*, Oxford University Press, 2002.

Dresser, Madge and Giles, Sue (eds.), *Bristol and Transatlantic Slavery*, Bristol Museums and Art Gallery and The University of the West of England, 2000.

Dunn, Richard S., *Sugar and Slaves: The Rise of the Planter Class in the West Indies, 1624–1713*, University of North Carolina, 1972.

Eickelmann, Christine and Small, David, *Pero: The Life of a Slave in Eighteenth-Century Bristol*, Redcliffe Press, 2004.

Eltis, David, *The Rise of African Slavery in the Americas*, Cambridge University Press, 2000.

Equiano, Olaudah, *Equiano's Travels*, edited by Paul Edwards, Heinemann, 1997.

Fisher, Humphrey J., *Slavery in the History of Muslim Black Africa*, New York University Press, 2001.

Fogel, Robert William and Engerman, Stanley, *Time on the Cross: Evidence and Methods – A Supplement*, Little Brown, 1974.

Fryer, Peter, *Staying Power: The History of Black People in Britain*, Pluto Press, 1984.

Geggus, David, *Slave Resistance Studies and the Saint Domingue Slave Revolt: Some Preliminary Considerations*, Florida International University, 1983.

Gifford, Zerbanoo, *Thomas Clarkson and the Campaign against Slavery*, Anti-Slavery International, 1996.

Gondola, Didier, *The History of the Congo*, Greenwood Press, 2002.

Gregory, Philippa, *A Respectable Trade*, Harper Collins, 1996.

Harris, Robert, *The Diligent: a Voyage Through the Worlds of the Slave Trade*, Perseus Press, 2002.

Hart, Richard, *Slaves who Abolished Slavery, Volume I – Blacks in Bondage*, University of the West Indies Press, 1980.

Hart, Richard, *Slaves who Abolished Slavery, Volume II – Blacks in Rebellion*, University of the West Indies Press, 1985, 2002.

Hayward, Jack (ed.), *Out of Slavery – Abolition and After: Legacies of West Indian Slavery*, Frank Cass, 1985.

Heuman, Gad, *The Caribbean*, Hodder Arnold, 2006.

Hill, Christopher, *Reformation to Industrial Revolution, Volume II: 1530–1780*, Penguin Books, 1969.

Hill, Clifford, *The Wilberforce Connection*, Monarch Books, 2004.

Hill, C.P., *British Social and Economic History, 1700–1982*, Edward Arnold, 1985.

Hobsbawm, F.J., *Industry and Empire: From 1750 to the Present Day*, Penguin, 1968.

Hochschild, Adam, *Bury the Chains: The British Struggle to Abolish Slavery*, Macmillan, 2005.

Hopkins, Dwight N. and Cummings, George (eds.), *Cut Loose Your Stammering Tongue: Black Theology in the Slave Narratives*, Orbis Books, 1991.

Hugill, Anthony, *Sugar and all that... A History of Tate and Lyle*, Gentry Books, 1978.

Hurmence, Belinda (ed.), *My folks don't want me to talk about slavery*, John F. Blair, 1984.

Inkori, Joseph E. and Engerman, Stanley L. (eds.), *The Atlantic Slave Trade*, Duke University Press, 1992.

Inikori, Joseph E., *Africans and the Industrial Revolution in England: A Study in International Trade and Economic Development*, University of Rochester, 2002.

James, C.L.R., *The Black Jacobins: Toussaint L'Ouverture and the San Domingo Revolution*, Alison & Busby, 1938.

Jordan, Winthrop D., *White over Black: American Attitudes Toward the Negro 1550–1812*, University of North Carolina, 1968.

Jordan, Winthrop D., *The White Man's Burden: Historical Origins of Racism in the United States*, Oxford University Press, 1974.

Kanneh, Kadiatu, *African Identities: Race, Nation and Culture in Ethnography, Pan-Africanism and Black Literatures*, Routledge, 1998.

Klein, Herbert S., *The Atlantic Trade*, Cambridge University Press, 1999.

Knight, Franklin W., *The Caribbean: The Genesis of a Fragmented Nationalism*, Oxford University Press, 1978.

Kohn, Marek, *The Race Gallery: the Return of Racial Science*, Jonathan Cape, 1995.

Kolchin, Peter, *American Slavery: 1619–1877*, Hill and Wang, 1994.

Koslow, Philip, *Centuries of Greatness, The West African Kingdoms: 750–1900*, Chelsea House Publishers, 1995.

Long, Edward, *The History of Jamaica*, Ian Randle, 2003.

Lovejoy, Paul E., *Transformations in Slavery: A History of Slavery in Africa*, Cambridge University Press, 1983.

Lowenthal, David, *West Indian Societies*, Oxford University Press, 1972.

Malouf, Amin, *Leo the African*, Abacus Books, 1994.

Manning, Patrick, *Slavery and African Life*, Cambridge University Press, 1990.

Mellon, James (ed.), *Bullwhip Days: the Slaves Remember – An Oral History*, Grove Press, 1988.

Midgley, Clare, *Women Against Slavery: The British Campaigns 1780–1870*, Routledge, 1992.

Moron, Guillermo, *A History of Venezuela*, George Allen and Unwin, 1964.

Munson, James, *The Nonconformists: in Search of a Lost Culture*, SPCK, 1991.

Nwachukwu, Frank Ukadike, *Black African Cinema*, University of California Press, 1994.

Oliver, Roland and Fage, J.D., *A Short History of Africa*, Pelican Books, 1988.

Parry, J.H., Sherlock, Philip and Maingot, Anthony, *A Short History of the West Indies*, Macmillan, 1987.

Pérez, Joseph, *La Emancipación en Hispanoamérica*, Sarpe, 1986.

Pérez, Louis A. Jnr., *Cuba: Between Reform and Revolution*, Oxford University Press, 1988.

Phillips, Caryl (ed.), *Extravagant Strangers: A Literature of Belonging*, Faber and Faber, 1997.

Pinn, Anthony B., *Terror and Triumph: The Nature of Black Religion*, Fortress Press, 2003.

Pollock, John, *John Wesley*, Lion, 1989.

Pollock, John, *Wilberforce*, Lion, 1977.

Pope-Hennessy, James, *Sins of the Father: The Atlantic Slave Traders 1441–1807*, Castle Books, 2004.

Ramsay, James, *An Essay on the Treatment and Conversion of African Slaves in the British Sugar Colonies*, J. Phillips, 1784.

Rodney, Walter, *How Europe Underdeveloped Africa*, Bogle L'Ouverture, 1972.

Ross, Andrew, *David Livingstone: Mission and Empire*, Hambledon & London, 2002.

Rudé, George, *Hanoverian London: 1714–1808*, Sutton Publishing, 2003.

Schama, Simon, *Rough Crossings: Britain, the Slaves and the American Revolution*, BBC Books, 2005.

Scott, Anne, *Hannah More: The First Victorian*, Oxford University Press, 2003

Segal, Ronald, *Islam's Black Slaves: The History of Africa's Other Black Diaspora*, Atlantic Books. 2001,

Segal, Ronald, *The Race War: The Worldwide Conflict of Races*, Penguin. 1967,

Smith, Adam, *An Inquiry into the Nature and Causes of the Wealth of the Nations*, edited by Edwin Cannan, Random House, 1994.

Smith, M.G., *The Plural Society in the British West Indies*, Sangster's & University of California Press, 1974.

St Clair, William, *The Grand Slave Emporium: Cape Coast Castle and the British Slave Trade*, Profile Books, 2006.

Sturge, Joseph and Harvey, Thomas, *The West Indies in 1837*, Hamilton, Adams, & Co., 1838.

Thomas, Hugh, *The Slave Trade: The Story of the Atlantic Slave Trade 1440–1870*, Touchstone, 1997.

Tomkins, Stephen, *John Wesley: A Biography*, Lion, 2003.

Van Sertima, Ivan, *They Came Before Columbus: The African Presence in Ancient America*, Random House, 1976.

Walker, Robin, *When We Ruled*, Every Generation Media, 2006.

Walvin, James, *An African's Life: The Life and Times of Olaudah Equiano, 1745–1797*, Continuum, 1998.

Walvin, James, *Black Ivory: Slavery in the British Empire*, Blackwell, 2001.

Ware, Vron, *Beyond the Pale: White Women, Racism and History*, Verso, 1992.

Williams, Eric, *Capitalism and Slavery*, Andre Deutsch, 1964.

Williams, Eric, *From Columbus to Castro: The History of the Caribbean*, Andre Deutsch, 1970.

Wollstonecraft, Mary, *A Vindication of the Rights of Woman*, Cambridge University Press, 1995.

Wood, Donald, *Trinidad in Transition: The Years After Slavery*, Oxford University Press, 1968.

Act to end slavery now, Anti-Slavery International and set all free, 2006.

Slavery and Abolition – *A Journal of Slave and Post Slave Studies*; 'Special Issue: Unfree Labour in the Development of the Atlantic World', edited by Gad Heuman and James Walvin, Frank Cass, Volume 14, Number 2, August 1993.

Slavery and Abolition – *A Journal of Slave and Post Slave Studies*: 'Vagrancy, Impressment and Regulation of Labour in Eighteenth Century Britain', edited by Paul E. Lovejoy and Nicholas Rogers, Frank Cass, Volume 15, Number 2, August 1994.

Index

William Wilberforce
A Biography
Stephen Tomkins

In the 1780s, 40,000 slaves a year were taken from Africa in British ships, on the notorious Middle Passage, to the Caribbean. In 1787, under an oak tree in Kent, the Prime Minister William Pitt invited his friend William Wilberforce to bring a bill before the House of Commons, outlawing the slave trade. Neither of them imagined a 20-year political campaign, which consumed the rest of Wilberforce's life and finally led the slaves to sing, 'Oh, me good friend, Mr Wilberforce, make we free! God Almighty thank ye!'

Born in Hull to wealthy middle-class parents, Wilberforce entered parliament aged just 21 and soon became a political celebrity of his day. During the 1780s, he underwent a profound Christian conversion and set out on the path of service to humanity. Tomkins charts his battle to end the slave trade, portraying a man of contradictions and extraordinary determination.

Drawing extensively on eyewitness testimonies about slavery and the slave trade, and written in a lively and engaging style, this book transports the reader back to a dramatic age of conflict and upheaval. It brings Wilberforce and an extensive cast of colourful characters vividly to life.

ISBN 978-0-7459-5232-1